THE NEW
THRACIAN
TREASURE
FROM ROGOZEN, BULGARIA

THE NEW
THRACIAN
TREASURE
FROM ROGOZEN, BULGARIA

A.Fol   B.Nikolov   R.F.Hoddinott

Published for the Trustees of the British Museum
by British Museum Publications

Published by British Museum Publications Limited
46 Bloomsbury Street, London WC1B 3QQ

British Library Cataloguing in Publication Data

The new Thracian treasure from Rogozen, Bulgaria.
1. Material culture—Thrace—Exhibitions
2. Thrace—Antiquities—Exhibitions
I. Fol, Alexander II. Nikolov, Bogdan
III. Hoddinott, R.F.
939'.8   DR50.43

ISBN 0-7141-1290-9

Designed by Adrian Hodgkins
Set in Photina and printed in Great Britain by
A. Wheaton & Co. Ltd, Marsh Barton, Exeter, Devon

Contents

Acknowledgements

The Lyudmila Zhivkova International Foundation
and The Trustees of the British Museum gratefully
acknowledge the generous assistance
of the following:

Pergamon Group of Companies
Plessey UK Ltd
ICI PLC
John Brown PLC
Rank Xerox Ltd
Bulk Oil UK Ltd
Courtaulds Fibres Exports Ltd
Philipp Brothers
Raxvale Ltd
ICL
Schweppes International Ltd
Wogen Anniversary Trust
ISA Holdings Ltd
Marconi Instruments

Foreword

The Trustees of the British Museum are honoured to display the exhibition of the new Thracian treasure from Rogozen, presented by the Bulgarian Committee for Culture and the Lyudmila Zhivkova International Foundation. It includes material of the highest archaeological and mythological importance, and is all the more exciting for being shown so soon after its discovery. Special thanks are due to Mr Vladimir Zhivkov, President, and Dr Ivan Nedev, Secretary General of the Lyudmila Zhivkova International Foundation; to Dr Roumen Katincharov, Director General of the State Amalgamation 'Cultural and Historic Heritage'; to Dr G. Lasov, the Commissar for the exhibition; to Professor A. Fol and Dr V. Nikolov, who wrote the catalogue with its Bulgarian introduction, and to Mr R. F. Hoddinott, who contributed the English introduction. We are also greatly indebted to the Bulgarian Ambassador in London, His Excellency Mr Kiril Shterev, to the Bulgarian Cultural Councillor, Dr P. Shopov, to the Press Attaché, Mr P. Voinovsky, and to the staff of the British Embassy in Sofia. The exhibition would scarcely have been possible without the support of Mr Robert Maxwell, Chairman of the Lyudmila Zhivkova International Foundation (England and Wales). The Keeper of Greek and Roman Antiquities in the British Museum, Mr B. F. Cook, has been responsible for the exhibition on the British side, and specialised help has been given by Mr G. House, Head of Public Services in the Museum, by Mr I. D. Jenkins of the Department of Greek and Roman Antiquities, by Mr N. Grant of Mirror Group Newspapers and by the British Museum's Design Section and Public Relations Office. Following the very successful exhibition of Thracian Treasures from Bulgaria at the British Museum in 1976, which was opened by the late Lyudmila Zhivkova, this exhibition is a further example of the desire of both Britain and Bulgaria to foster cultural relations, and may also be seen as a tribute to Lyudmila Zhivkova's memory.

Windlesham
Chairman of the Trustees
of the British Museum

Preface

It is an honour for me to present to the British public, and to academic and cultural circles, this catalogue of the exhibition, *The New Thracian Treasure from Rogozen, Bulgaria.*

It is organised by the Bulgarian Committee for Culture and the Lyudmila Zhivkova International Foundation, with the kind assistance of the Chairman of the UK Branch of the Foundation, Mr Robert Maxwell, MC, of our hosts, Sir David Wilson, the Director of the British Museum and Mr Brian Cook, Keeper of Greek and Roman Antiquities, and of leading companies and citizens of this country.

The Rogozen find is a wonderful example of Thracian art. It is remarkable not only in quantity but also for the superb workmanship of the ancient craftsmen who lived in our lands. It is a fact of history that 'the most numerous people in the world after the Indians', as Herodotus described the Thracians, have produced works of creative craftsmanship bearing the mark of eternity.

The memory of the Bulgarian lands is ancient and powerful. They were a crossroads and focus of civilisations and cultures, a home of values of universal significance. It gives me pleasure to point out that their excavation, preservation and popularisation is a constant responsibility of socialist culture in Bulgaria. 'We cherish as our sacred heritage everything that immortalises the creative genius, the art and optimism of our ancestors', said Todor Zhivkov, President of the State Council of the People's Republic of Bulgaria, 'and it is our duty to hand it on to future generations.'

The current exhibition is another example of fruitful Anglo-Bulgarian cultural exchange, and offers experts and connoisseurs a fine opportunity to experience once again the excitement of an encounter with one of the oldest cultures in Europe. It is a continuation of the exhibition of Thracian Treasures from Bulgaria opened at the British Museum ten years ago by Bulgaria's remarkable daughter, Lyudmila Zhivkova.

Great cultural achievements are the most eloquent testimony for the permanence of Creation. Synonymous with progress and the essence of civilisation, culture is a solid bridge which carries the most noble impulses for peace, progress, harmony and perfection.

We would like to believe that this exhibition, another celebration of man's creativity, will help our nations to learn more about each other, and will strengthen trust and friendship between them in a peaceful world.

Georgi Yordanov
*Deputy Chairman of the Council of Ministers of
The People's Republic of Bulgaria
Chairman of The Council for Science, Culture and
Education*

**Map showing find-spots of
Thracian antiquities**

1. Iron Gates
2. Poroina
3. Peretu
4. Agighiol
5. Yakimovo
6. Bukuovtsi
7. Sofronievo
8. Galiche
9. Rogozen
10. Belene
11. Borovo

12. Gurchinovo
13. Branichevo
14. Vratsa
15. Vladinya
16. Vulchi Trun
17. Loukovit
18. Letnitsa
19. Vurbitsa
20. Radyuvene (Stoyanovo)
21. Kazichene (Sofia)
22. Strelcha

23. Panagyurishte
24. Douvanli
25. Rozovets
26. Dulboki
27. Daskal Atanasovo
28. Brezovo
29. Priboi
30. Mezek
31. Alexandrovo

Introduction

The Thracian silver treasure unearthed at the village of Rogozen (Vratsa District, north-western Bulgaria) was immediately hailed as a 'sensational find' by newsmen, but actually it was not very surprising. The treasure fits perfectly onto the archaeological map of north-central and north-western Thrace south of the Danube, an area from which had come most of the previously known vessels of silver, silver-gilt and gold that range in date from the mid-second to the end of the first millennium BC. The initial inspection of the objects at the time of their discovery showed that they support existing hypotheses on Thracian cosmogony, mythology, religion and culture.

The Rogozen treasure, however, was assembled between the last quarter of the fifth century and approximately the 340s BC. The information gleaned from it, including Greek inscriptions with Thracian personal and place names now found for the first time in any quantity, covers a long period. The wealth of material now available is making even more complex the questions raised in earlier studies and has opened up the subject for further research to an unexpected and exciting degree. This is perhaps the real 'sensation'.

The problems associated with the Rogozen treasure can be broken down into three overlapping fields of study. The first is concerned with Thracian history; the second with poorly-documented connections within the contact areas of south-eastern Europe; and the third with the particular issues that arise out of an illiterate culture and broaden into the general problems of Indo-European (and, for that matter, Indo-Iranian) linguistics.

To deal first with historical questions. The Rogozen treasure has confirmed the unpopular view that precious metal was mined and processed in the area of north-western Thrace south of the Danube as well as in Transylvania and Pangeus. We need the results of sampling before conjecturing where the ore was found. Samples are now required from river beds and ancient veins in spurs of the Balkan range, which have been previously disregarded. Here, as elsewhere, the metal was mined and processed under control i.e. under a centralised monopoly. In the early Thracian social structure, which was organised in a two-tier pattern (a clan-society followed later by a ter-ritorial social structure), the so-called 'royal' economy now appears to have been much more developed than hitherto supposed. Signs of such an economy were looked for in the south-east, in the Propontis (Sea of Marmara) area, where indeed it might have been expected. Now, however, it seems that this type of slave-owning society may have extended to the north-east as well. This hypothesis requires a complete reappraisal of the economic role of slavery in Thracian society, which was previously thought to be only slightly developed. The most detailed Rogozen inscription (No. 29) includes a previously unknown Thracian personal name DISLOYAS, the name of the silversmith who made the *phiale*. This *phiale* originated in Beos, a Thracian site of uncertain location, which was already known from inscriptions on other vessels. The *phiale* had belonged to Kotys an Odrysian king who reigned between 383 and 359 BC. From this we may infer that a workshop for vessels in precious metal had been established in the settlement of Beos, under the Odrysian king's control.

The view common among historians that independent craftsmen travelled from place to place offering their skills wherever they were needed is no longer applicable to studies on Thracian antiquity. As demonstrated by the inscriptions on Thracian vessels from Rogozen, Borovo and the Mogilanska mound, as well as by those on individual *phialae* from the tombs at Agighiol, near Tulca in Romania, and in the Alexandrovo-Lovetch and Branitchevo-Shumen Districts in Bulgaria, royal workshops were established in several villages: Beos, Apros, Ergiske (also Argiske), Geistoi and Sauthaba. All of them have been identified – some positively, others with varying degrees of certainty – near the confluence of the Tonzos (Tundzha) and Hebros (Maritsa) rivers together with the adjacent Strandzha mountain massif and with the northern hinterland of Propontis.

The Odrysian kings in the fifth and the fourth centuries BC did not maintain a capital city. Following a practice known in other kingdoms also, they travelled from one fortified residence to another, as recorded in historical sources, exercising their military, political, economic and royal-cum-priestly authority as they went. This touring, which in practice was never discontinued, was ideologically justified in the spirit of the most ancient Indo-Iranian traditions. Everything required for both practical and spiritual purposes was available within the fortifications – a royal headquarters, a sanctuary, a treasury, stores of food and arms, barracks, stables and workshops. Here the precious metal was turned into objects. It had come into the Odrysian treasury as both taxes and gifts from the Greek colonies along the northern coast of the Aegean and Propontis, as well as from allied and vassal kings and dynasts. Reports by Thucydides and Diodorus indicate that, at the end of the fifth and the beginning of the fourth century BC, annual revenue in the form of ingots, vessels and coins might have exceeded two tons.

We have no such data concerning northwestern Thrace. It is there, however, that the major tribe of the Triballi was to be found. The Triballian raids southwards and eastwards are characterised in the written sources as a 'holy terror', while the archaeological data, the numerous treasures and burial gifts found particularly in that area, support the idea of a tribal dynasty holding both military and political power. It undoubtedly controlled both the mining and the processing of the rich ore deposits, and it is likely that it exported metal to its Odrysian allies in the south-east. The Triballian kings' residences have not yet been found, but the archaeological map suggests certain possibilities. It is probable, for instance, that the person buried in the so-called Mogilanska mound in Vratsa, where gold objects dating back to the first half of the fourth century BC were found, was a member of the Triballian dynasty.

The names of two of its kings are known from the written sources. The first is HALES, who attacked Abdera at the mouth of Nestos (Mesta) river in 376–5 BC. The second is SIRM, who faced Alexander the Great in a fierce battle in the Danube Plain in the spring of 335 BC and was repulsed, but not beaten. A previously unknown Thracian male name, DIDYKAIMOS, is legible on the rim of a *phiale* that bears a representation of the story of the priestess Auge and Herakles (No. 4). Could he have been a Triballian ruler?

The scanty information formerly available from the inscriptions on vessels from north and north-western Thrace south of the Danube has grown substantially, and the subject has become an important area of study. The data from the Rogozen inscriptions tell us that the Odrysian rulers bestowed diplomatic gifts on their worthiest and most sought-after allies. This sort of activity proved necessary in wars against Athens, who fought the Odrysians over the Thracian Chersonese (Gallipoli Peninsula) in the 370s and 360s BC, and against Philip II of Macedon, who invaded south-eastern Thrace in the 350s and 340s BC. Gifts came into the Triballian treasury from the Odrysian kings Satok (a Hellenised form of Sadok), a son of Sitalkes and a probable ruler after 424 BC (No. 27 and, probably, No. 118), Kotys I (see above) (Nos. 28, 30, 31, 40, 41, 42, 43, 45, 46 and 47), and his son Kersebleptes, a Hellenised form of Kersobleptes (No. 44), who ruled from 359 to 341 BC.

The history of the Triballi and of Triballian-Odrysian relations awaits further research.

Second, the question of contact overseas. A large number of the vessels were obviously produced by a workshop located somewhere in north-western Thrace south of the Danube. In addition to the gifts in the Rogozen treasure, however, there are some vessels made by Greek craftsmen or by Anatolian craftsmen in the Greek style; a third group has north Thracian motifs; and a fourth has motifs of the so-called 'Celtic' type.

The problems associated with the contact areas are rather difficult to deal with, while very little stylistic and typological analysis has yet been undertaken on the scenes, shapes, colours, decoration and methods of workmanship of the vessels. It is likely that the results of this sort of analysis will bring about some sort of re-evaluation of present ideas on the subject.

To set a clearer picture of the actual historical situation around 400–350 BC, let us look at the vessels simultaneously in the light of the inscriptions on them and of the ethno-political map of Thrace. The Rogozen inscriptions prove that the Graeco-Thracian contact area was split into two parts. Greece was maintaining contact both with north-western Thrace through the valleys of the Struma-Mesta rivers, and with eastern areas through the confluence of the Maritsa and Tundzha rivers. Their main area of contact centred on the Propontis area, since there were

Thracians on both shores, and it has been suggested that the workshops that produced most of the goods for the Thracian market were situated there. This theory has been corroborated by vessels in the Rogozen treasure of Greek and Anatolian origin, and in particular seems to be confirmed by the *phiale* with the scene of Auge and Herakles, as the hero seducing the priestess was of Anatolian-Mysian rather than 'European-Mysian' i.e. Thracian origin.

The Greek language spread slowly through the Graeco-Thracian contact area. This diffusion now appears for the first time to have spanned the south-eastern and eastern flanks of the country. All inscriptions, bar that on the *phiale* belonging to Didykaimos, originated from the Odrysian territories. Idiosyncracies in the use of Greek (including mistakes in copying the brief texts) in vessels from Rogozen and elsewhere can be used as evidence that a local patois expressing current political and ideological aims developed in Thrace at about this time. The nature of such a language, its pronunciation and exactly who spoke it are questions of particular interest in a completely illiterate society.

European and Anatolian Thrace constituted a second contact area independent of Greek cities, markets and workshops. The network of trade by land and sea together with a common linguistic and ethnic background led to a direct exchange of people, ideas and objects. All motifs and objects that can most readily be characterised as oriental came unimpeded and were readily assimilated into Thracian culture. The pattern worked in much the same way in the north and the north-east, and not just because the Danube, with tribes of Getai living on both banks, was not a barrier. The real explanation is to be found in the ethno-cultural and linguistic unity of the population of the Lower Danube area.

Proceeding north-eastwards, we enter the contact area between Thracians and Scythians. Its network of land and water routes acted as a reliable passage for intensive trade, interchange of ideas and often for military and political conflict. The history of these relations is too lengthy to be traced in detail here, but following the discovery of the Rogozen treasure one correction is necessary. It was formerly thought that Scythian contacts with the Thracians in the fifth and fourth

centuries BC were predominantly with the Odrysians. Contact between the Scythians and the Triballi (and, for that matter, with the Getai) do not fit into that pattern and require further research. I am convinced that a thorough investigation of this subject would point towards the concept of a Thracian-Scythian *koine* on the eve of the Hellenistic age.

Lastly, the Rogozen treasure has for the first time raised the question of Thracian-Celtic contact before what was presumed to be a devastating invasion. This possibility is suggested to me by the so-called 'Celtic' decorative motifs with (decapitated) human heads. These are found on five *phialae* from the Rogozen treasure (Nos. 99 to 103), but they cannot be linked either to the actual presence of Celts, or to direct Celtic influence. This means that all apparent Celtic influence on Thracian craftwork in the third century BC must now be reassessed. It is likely that the Danube and the roads running north-west along it formed the basis of the contact area, which doubtless extended much further.

The third question, dealing with an ancient illiterate culture, might be reduced to this: what is actually seen by an observer of an ancient object, an image or a structure? This question 'has recently been addressed by Bulgarian historians making use of the information provided by Thracian archaeological material.

A basic Thracian creation myth perceived the Great Mother-Goddess as a self-conceived being, who gave birth to a son (the Sun), waited for him to grow to manhood and then coupled with him to continue Nature's cycle of birth and renewal. A pair of quadrigae are shown on one of the jugs (No. 157 – the masterpiece of the treasure). Some commentators see a single goddess in each quadriga together with a female charioteer, while others prefer to interpret the two figures as a goddess and a male deity. The question, therefore, is whether these two figures represent the Great Mother-Goddess under two aspects, in her role as 'the origin' and at her son's holy investiture, or show instead the mother and her son in motion along the heavenly holy circle, parallel to that of the earth? Either option is possible in Thracian religious belief according to my hypothesis on Thracian Orphism.

The general view is that Thracian Orphism arose out of the intervention of the cosmological model of the world and the moral one. According to that view, an initiate (i.e. one chosen by virtue of his class status) could become immortal provided he had constantly striven towards perfection. Such a faith was appropriate for an illiterate society and differed radically from the Greek, which professed the immortality of the soul; here religious instruction was performed both via the oral poetic tradition and through sacred objects and buildings. In Thrace that sort of poetic tradition was reproduced on objects and structures, mostly in stylised scenes, but was inherent in their design as well. The poetic tradition was a royal one. In the social system where the integrity of society depended on that ideological convention, only the king was held to embody the perfection towards which the ordinary man strove. Ideological control over the enslaved and the underprivileged was therefore exerted by the king playing the dual role of both social and (according to mythological theory) cosmic mediator.

Scenes from the royal poetic tradition are shown on the Rogozen vessels. Most of them are known from other broadly similar representations, and have been excellently analysed. Every epic scene shows one of the tests the king had to pass before coupling ritually with the Great Mother-Goddess. Success in these tests involved a struggle encoded by various symbols. It has even been suggested that during the struggle the king was already formally recognised as a son of the Sun as well. A now famous text inscribed on the mouth of a silver-gilt ritual jug from Rogozen reads 'Kotys, son of Apollo' (No. 112). The Greek word used, *pais*, also means 'servant'. As suggested earlier, the king-god has indeed been found to be a priest of his cult. The inscription serves to corroborate fully the theory that Thracian Orphic teaching differed from the classical Greek mystical and idealistical Orphism in the fifth and the fourth centuries BC and later.

The Rogozen vessels will provide a key to a long closed door: how did Thracian mythological thinking translate into ritual practice, i.e. how did the doctrine of immortality affect behaviour? Behind that door also remains the mystery of buried treasure itself. Why is there so much buried treasure in Thrace, if, as is currently thought, it was buried by fugitives? It seems very unlikely that there would have been so many fugitives. For the moment at least, I suggest that the burials were carried out not as a temporary expedient, but quite deliberately as part of a religious ritual.

It is this theory that poses new problems and opens up new areas for research. It leads from particular to general questions connected with the four models of the world (cosmological, mythological, religious and social) among the nomadic peoples of the Black Sea area. Similarities and distinctions are both so increasingly clear-cut and positive that they point towards the need for joint research. Is is clear, to Bulgarian scholars at least, that the need for such research is urgent, not only at the level of direct comparison of data categories but also at the level of a cultural and historical synthesis applied in an ethnic, typological and geographic pattern.

Professor Alexander Fol
Doctor of History

Thracian Silver Treasure
from Rogozen

The largest known Thracian treasure dating back to the pre-Hellenistic period was discovered early in 1986. The treasure was found near the centre of the village of Rogozen, Vratsa District, in an empty plot that had for years been used as a vegetable garden.

The objects had been buried in two groups, in a pair of separate but adjacent pits. The first group of items was uncovered quite by chance by the owner of the plot, a tractor driver called Ivan Dimitrov. He was digging a trench for a waterpipe in his garden when, at a depth of some 40 to 50 cm, he found sixty-five silver vessels, which he turned over to the Vratsa District Museum of History. The museum immediately appointed a team of archaeologists who, under Dr Bogdan Nikolov, a senior research associate with the Museum, started rescue excavations where the treasure had been discovered. The archaeologists' aim was to find out whether it was part of some Thracian burial or an early settlement, and to establish the reasons for its burial in the first place.

After several days' hard work, an archaeological sounding was made. First the initial find pit was fully excavated and then the area of excavation was extended in all directions. It became obvious that there was no sign either of an ancient settlement or of a burial. The treasure had therefore been hidden at a time of great danger. The archaeologists had no idea at this time that the precious items had been buried in two separate groups, and proceeded with their work accordingly in spite of the wintry conditions. On 6 January 1986 their efforts were finally rewarded. At a distance of 5 metres north-east of the first pit, a second was uncovered containing precisely one hundred items.

The Rogozen treasure is made up of 165 silver vessels, of which 31 are gilded. They weigh 20 kilos in total and were made of high quality silver. The vessels can be divided into three groups: 108 bowls (*phialae*), 54 jugs and 3 cups. This is the largest Thracian treasure to be discovered in Bulgaria. It is also the first to be recovered by archaeologists, and therefore of particular importance. To date, no fewer than ten Thracian treasures have been found in the middle of northern Bulgaria: at Valtchitran and Belene (Pleven District); at Vladinya, Letnitsa, Lukovit and Radyuvene (Lovetch District); at Borovo

(Russe District); at Yakimovo (Mikhailovgrad District); at Vukyovtsi and Galitche (Vratsa District). A Thracian gold treasure has been found at Panagyurishte.

All were buried at a time of great danger. The exact location of the sites where these treasures were found is unclear, and the precise nature of the finds themselves remains unknown. It is impossible to tell what proportion of the material found was turned over to the museums, and what might have been missed by the untrained eye, as the treasures were dug up without any expert help or supervision.

The Rogozen treasure is likely to have belonged to a wealthy Thracian ruling family. The items were obviously accumulated over several generations, from the end of the fifth until the middle of the fourth century BC. Their splendour and magnificence accords with the idea of a Thracian aristocracy aspiring to manifest both power and authority through wealth and opulence. The objects were made at the height of the flowering of Thracian culture, at a time when Thracian political influence was at its most potent in the Balkans. In the fifth and fourth centuries BC the Thracian kings sought to establish a single empire along the lines of the Persian one. Thrace's commercial and cultural links with the lands of both the Levant and the Black Sea hinterland soon turned it into a major cultural centre and during this time Thrace grew in stature until it surpassed the people of mid- and western Europe in economic, political and cultural development.

So why was the Rogozen treasure buried at all? The explanation probably lies in a series of military campaigns and incursions that took place over the lands of the Triballi in the second half of the fourth century BC. These understandably led to a general sense of insecurity among the Thracian population, as the foreign armies plundered freely. The most famous of these campaigns were conducted by the kings of Macedon, Philip II and Alexander the Great. It was against this background that the last owner of the Rogozen treasure split the silver vessels into two groups, put them in a pair of bags made of some non-durable material and buried them in two shallow adjacent pits. The Thracian's fate is unknown to us, but we can assume that he was either killed or taken prisoner. Thus the precious silver items came to remain undisturbed in the ground for more than 2,300 years.

Phialae constitute the largest share of silver vessels in the Rogozen treasure. There are 108 altogether. This is more than twice the number known in the world's museums. The exceptionally wide range of *phialae* in the Rogozen treasure enables us to identify those imported or manufactured after foreign models and those from established local workshops. The word *phiale* was a Greek one, meaning a kind of shallow cup with a semispherical boss (an *omphalos* or an umbo) in the centre at the base. Ancient Greeks, Thracians, Persians, Scythians and Romans used *phialae* for libations or for feasting. *Phialae* are therefore often encountered both in the Near East or the Aegean area and in the lands of the Thracians and the Scythians. The earliest *phiale* found in Bulgaria was of bronze. It has been dated through the inventory of a seventh-century BC burial, discovered at Sofronievo (Vratsa District).

The Rogozen treasure *phialae* were made by various hands and in various workshops in ancient Thrace. They were hammered out of silver sheets onto prepared matrices. After this the decoration would be completed by chasing and chiselling with special tools. The ornament on some of the vessels is extremely delicate and quite spectacular.

The Rogozen *phialae* can be divided into three main types: dish-like, cup-like and ordinary.

The last type includes the most varieties. They differ from one another in decoration generally and in the detail of particular patterns. Dish-like *phialae* are simpler. Ornament is either geometric or floral, for instance the solid silver *phiale* with lotus-blossom decoration (No. 2). Parallels exist in the lands of ancient Colchis, where gold pieces dating back to the fourth century BC have been found and similar examples are known from both northern Dobrudzha and Macedonia. An interesting scene of classical Greek mythology is rendered on one dish-like *phiale*: the figures of Herakles and Auge, princess of Teheya (No. 4), are raised in high relief. A Greek text *Avge Delade* is inscribed above the characters' heads and the Thracian personal name *Didykaimo* (genitive of DIDYKAIMOS) is inscribed with dotted lines on the rim.

There are twenty-one cup-like *phialae* in the Rogozen treasure (Nos. 5–25 incl.). These are small deep vessels of globular body, with a short neck and a boss in the centre of the base. The rims are pronounced and almost all of them are undecorated. The silversmith expressed his aesthetic concept in the elegant outline.

Ordinary shallow *phialae* are the most common. Nearly all of them are decorated and display an unusual degree of ornamentation, as well as ingenious decorative patterns. More of this type appear in the Rogozen treasure for the first time. *Phialae* with decoration consisting of fluting, ovolo and beading arranged radially around the boss are typical. Thracian craftsmen's preference for combining geometric patterns with floral motifs can be seen where a stylised palmette, a lotus-blossom, an acorn, an almond, an ivy-sprig and a fir-cone are worked together. It is possible that each motif had some symbolic connotation, but we have no means of interpreting them.

Phialae with combined animal and floral ornament deserve special attention. Two *phialae* are decorated with bovine heads alternating with acorns (Nos. 94 and 95). On another *phiale* a raised lion-griffin image is seen, framed by a band of lotus-blossom and seven stylised birds (No. 96). The lion-griffin image is unique in its iconography and the birds are similar to those on the bronze matrix found at Gartchinovo (Targovishte District). No doubt, these images were the outcome of a very ancient local tradition and were manufactured in Thracian workshops. However it is obvious that some of the *phialae* were made either under Oriental influence or imported direct. A *phiale* decorated with four pairs of griffins (No. 97) is an example of this.

One pair of exquisitely made silver *phialae* from the Rogozen treasure are decorated with bands of human heads in relief. On the first there are eight female heads (No. 99) which are identical both in size and technique. They display a young female face with large eyes and a tiny mouth. Above the forehead the hair is plaited in three braids falling loosely beside the face. The calm expression on the face, the way the hair is treated and the spirituality all recall certain motifs on jugs from the Rogozen treasure. The ornamental composition of the second *phiale* is almost identical (No. 100). Here the human heads are seven in number and are hammered in the same way. The distinction lies in the hair-styles, which here appear as a pair of large twisted locks curling at the ends and beside the ears. The eyebrows are bushy and the eyes are unnaturally large. The expression is not friendly. The faces probably represent two different deities from the Thracian pantheon. The same applies to the decoration of four other *phialae*. Each has a head of a deity in relief soldered to the inside, on the boss (Nos. 101–104). These heads are almost identical and are shown as though they were looking at the onlooker. The faces are youthful with fluffy hair.

Some more archaic types are also present among the *phialae* of the Rogozen treasure. They fall into the category of dish-like *phialae* or into the ordinary category of undecorated *phialae*. Inscriptions in Greek appear on most of them. The characters are early and point to a date at the end of the fifth and beginning of the fourth century BC. The rest of the *phiale* types can be dated to the first half of the fourth century BC and not later than the 340s BC. There are no *phialae* of the Hellenistic period in the Rogozen treasure.

Jugs are the next major group. They number fifty-four in all. These silver vessels, graceful both in shape and outline, have a singe flat upright ornate handle that ends below with either a stylised palmette or a human head in relief. The jugs fall into two types: they are either decorated with patternwork or show mythological scenes. An earlier type has scant geometric decoration on the shoulder only. A complete series of types and varieties is displayed by jugs with geometric ornaments. Rings and bands of ovolo, fluting, raised beading and incision are all to be found. The Thracian craftsmen seem to be in pursuit of great variety and rhythm. Floral motifs combine with the geometric patterns and in the decoration of both *phialae* and jugs, ivy and palmettes are mixed (No. 119). One can see how symbolism brought motif stylisation to an abstract level in an ingenious design (Nos. 119, 143–53).

Geometric, floral and stylised animal motifs in the decoration of jugs all resulted from an established local tradition of Thracian metalwork. When taken together, the jugs of that type represent a particular branch of Thracian goldsmiths' work. It seems that Thracian craftsmen produced work that their customers liked and in

turn tailored their output to meet their customers' requirements.

The Rogozen silver jugs, which carry representations both of deities and of cult scenes, were dependent on certain rules as well as on a strictly established stylistic iconography. Their iconographic images and patterns were well known to the Thracian goldsmiths. They understood them thoroughly and produced specimens in precious metal to use as models. A canonical tradition specified both which image should be seen where and what else should be shown with it. With the next group of jugs, therefore, we shall see how the goldsmith unfolded the story and how everything was set in its right place. In representing Thracian or Greek myths, certain conventions of posture, action and expressions had to be followed. The myths were always presented in the same way so that they were immediately recognisable to the customer or onlooker. Both would have been fully aware of the mythology and all the associated images. The next group of Rogozen jugs all share this common stylistic background.

There are nine silver jugs that have cult scenes with deities and their attributes on them. One of them shows a Greek myth, the rest treat subjects from the Thracian pantheon. Until recently, anthropomorphic images on Thracian works of art dating back to the pre-Hellenistic age were non-existent. In recent years a find at Bovoro (Russe District) has produced some more.

The only Rogozen jug with a Greek myth shows a scene from Herakles' Ninth Labour (No. 154). The figures of Herakles and Hippolyta, Queen of the Amazons, were hammered in low relief over a prepared matrix. Behind them are a lion-griffin and a horse. The composition is nicely calculated – human and animal figures are repeated three times in the same form around the surface of the jug. It seems that in spite of a tendency to imitate classical Greek art, the Thracian craftsman had not quite succeeded in rendering everything accurately. Both the posture and the gestures of the figures are slightly unnatural and naive. Their faces and hair-styles are entirely alike and they have obviously been impressed from the same templates. None of this is normal in classical Greek art and so it becomes apparent that the jug is the work of a Thracian craftsman. Scenes derived from the myth of Herakles and the Amazons are not without precedent in Thracian art: they have frequently been encountered on objects found in Thrace.

The next eight jugs present Thracian myths. The images and the cult scenes refer to at least two deities of the Thracian pantheon. Very little is known about the deities in the early period of Thracian art because finds of relevant material have been few. Later representations of the deities are found much more often on finds from the Late Roman period in Thrace, although these later images are unfortunately somewhat lacking in authority. The Rogozen treasure helps to correct this imbalance by providing a wealth of material showing characters and scenes from the fifth and fourth centuries BC.

The first four jugs show images and scenes associated with the cult of the Great Goddess. The rest are concerned with a Thracian deity who is almost unknown in the early classical period. Most characteristic is the jug which shows the Great Goddess as a huntress, riding a lioness (No. 155). The goddess is moving to the right. With her right arm she grips the neck of her sacred animal while in her left hand she holds a bow and arrow. The goddess is bare-footed. Her hair is plaited in two layers of braids on her forehead and their ends fall unrestricted by her face. The goddess is turned towards the onlooker, with her face calm and bearing a majestic expression. She is dressed in an ankle-length *chiton*, with short sleeves. The dress is slung from the left shoulder and under her right armpit. The breasts of the goddess are not indicated and the folds of the dress are indicated by lines. The clothing of a goddess on the silver *rhyton* from Poroina (Romania) is shown in a similar way. The rider is shown in the same form on both sides of the Rogozen jug. She is moving to the right on one side and to the left on the other. Between the two images of the Great Goddess is a scene of a 'Lion Attacking a Stag'. Both animals move to the left. This is the first time that the Great Goddess is depicted as a huntress in early Thracian art. It could not have been the work of a Greek craftsman, because he would have given the goddess the appropriate Greek clothing and attributes. The image of the Great Goddess on the lioness shows signs of the excellent training that is known quite early in local Thracian art. One gets the impression that a very skilled craftsman was at work on a subject wholly familiar to him.

Both faces of the next jug display the scene of the 'Lion Attacking A Hind' (No. 156). The animals are correctly rendered anatomically and are more or less in proportion. Similar scenes of animal subjects are already known from the treasures from Vratsa (Fig. 3) and Lukovit and from the appliqués of the Letnitsa Treasure. They are shown on appliqués which are of some importance. On the Rogozen jug the subject is rendered quite realistically and accurately. Its appearance alongside the Great Goddess as a huntress explains both the concept and the meaning of the whole scene and is useful for putting an end to speculation on the matter.

On the next jug we are faced with a quite unexpected scene, which is probably associated with the same cult. On a wide frieze a pair of four-wheeled chariots (No. 157) are shown. Four winged horses are harnessed to each chariot. The chariots themselves are also winged, as are the chariots on the gold jug from the Mogilanska mound (Vratsa). The two female charioteers look much the same. Their clothing is identical. In one of the chariots the Great Goddess is seated on a high cushioned chair. She is holding a sprig in her right hand and a deep *phiale* in her left. In the second chariot the Great Goddess is seen again, this time as a huntress with a bow and arrow. It is undoubtedly the same goddess in both chariots, shown in her two roles. Similar images of a goddess (there interpreted as Artemis) in a chariot are known in Greece but date to an earlier period. As a mistress of the plant kingdom, she holds the same flowering sprigs as the second goddess in these chariots, but the Greek scene is associated with the goddess Artemis as well.

Until now only assumptions and theories have existed about the Great Goddess of the Thracians, some more likely than others. Thrace poses numerous puzzles and the Great Goddess is but one of them. This has partially been relieved by the Rogozen discovery as we now have at least some idea of the Thracian iconography for her. The images known previously, which date back to the fifth and fourth centuries BC, were all works by Greek artists and were found in Greece itself. In these the goddess was dressed in Greek clothing and assumed postures similar to those of the Greek deities. This was the image we had of her from a pair of reliefs found in the Piraeus, one in Copenhagen and the other in the British Museum (Fig. 10). In the Phillippi reliefs (of a later date) she is also holding a budded plant with a doe in front of her, but the image is still a Greek one and the concept includes the idea of Artemis as well. The Rogozen treasure shows a truly Thracian Great Goddess in an indigenous form for the first time.

On the next jug from the Rogozen treasure the Great Goddess is shown as a patroness of the animal world (No. 158). The images are depicted in two registers. In the upper register the Great Goddess occupies a central position. She is winged and in each hand holds a dog by its front paws. From both flanks a pair of centaur-like monsters rush towards her. They also are winged. On the lower register animals are shown in relief. A bull is attacked from each side by a pair of dogs. The sacred animals on the jug are rendered quite realistically, and are clearly defined. They complement the theme of the Great Goddess and fill out our concept of her.

The subjects on the next four jugs from the Rogozen treasure are all associated with the cult of another member of the Thracian pantheon. A rider holding a spear is shown on both sides of one jug and the riders are rushing towards each other (No. 159). A boar with a spear wound is shown between them. The 'Boar Hunt' theme has been examined and studied in depth. Its basic significance is now more or less clear and the representation of the scene on the Rogozen jug helps to clarify the ideas further. The theme is undisputedly a Thracian one. The image of the hunter-rider is a common one in Thrace in the fourth and third centuries BC.

On the next two jugs we are faced with a scene that is difficult to explain (Nos. 160 and 161). A bovine head and some scaly animals are displayed within a wide frieze on the body of the jug. The bovine head and horns are stylised to resemble an Ionic capital and the mane is rendered as a palmette. A similar image can be seen on an appliqué from the Letnitsa treasure, but we still do not know what it means.

There are Greek inscriptions on two jugs as well as on thirteen *phialae* in the Rogozen treasure. They include Thracian personal names as well as the names of five Thracian villages. The number of inscriptions is surprising, as hitherto fewer than

ten had been found in Bulgaria. Three *phialae* with identical inscriptions were found with a Thracian burial in the Mogilanska mound (Vratsa), one was found at Alexandrovo (Lovetch District), another in a mound grave at Branitchevo (Shumen District), and one in the Agighiol tomb in Northern Dobrudzha. One should also count a *phiale* in a private collection, found in the Lovetch area, which reads KOTYOS EKS GEYSTON.

Inscriptions on the *phialae* and jugs from the Rogozen treasure fall into two types. The first are inscriptions of Thracian personal names in the genitive like SATOKOY (No. 27) and DIDIKAYMO (No. 3), or in the nominative like KOTYS APOLLONOS PAIS, 'Kotys, son of Apollo'. The second type combines personal names of Thracian villages, including Beos (Nos. 28–9), Apros (Nos. 30–31), Sauthaba (No. 41), Ergiske (Nos. 43–4, also spelled Argiske on No. 42) and Geistoi (No. 46). The Rogozen inscriptions provide new data but raise new questions.

There are only three cups from the Rogozen treasure, but they are all of different shapes and types. They are all of high quality silver and gilded. The first one (No. 163), considered the earliest in date, was cast and is decorated with an ivy wreath. The cup originally had a pair of symmetrical upright handles, but these were lost before the treasure was buried. Both in shape and decoration, the cup is unique in Thrace.

The second cup is shaped like a classical *skyphos* (No. 164). It is decorated with a band of stylised palmettes and S-shaped motifs. There is a twenty-petalled rosette on its base. Its closest parallel is with the *skyphos* from Streltcha. The difference between them lies in their decoration. There are female heads, as well as rams' and lions' heads, on the Streltcha *skyphos*.

The third Rogozen cup is large and was hammered over a matrix from a thin sheet of silver. The images on it are in relief and the details are chased. The cup has an almost cylindrical shape, slightly narrower at the waist (No. 165). It was damaged before discovery. Nevertheless, the images are of particular interest. A continuous frieze of stylised antlers is raised below the rim. Each antler branch ends in a bird's head. On the body in low relief is a procession of animals including a billy-goat, some stags and a bird of prey. The bird is shown in side view and faces right. In its beak it clutches a fish which is covered with scales, with lines for the details of the tail and the fins. In its talons the bird clutches a hare, which has short ears and paws marked with strokes. Next to the bird, a winged billy-goat is shown moving to the right. Its horns are bent sharply backwards and its eye is big and round. In front of the goat is a stag, also seen in side view and moving to the right. All four legs are visible, but not the head as the cup is damaged there. The antlers of the stag are almost as long as its body and their branches point upwards.

At the very front of the procession walks an enormous stag with eight legs. The legs are seen from the side and move to the right. Its head is missing because of the damage. The base of the cup is framed by two rings of incisions and forms a tondo. In the centre of the tondo there is a scene of a 'Wolf Attacking a Boar'. The animals are seen from the side, moving to the right. The wolf has sprung onto its victim's back and has sunk its sharp claws into its body and bitten it through the ear. The beast has small pointed ears and a big elliptical eye. The fangs in its open mouth are shown by bands of incision. The boar's tusks are not depicted.

Three similar cups have been found in Romania. They also date back to the first half of the fourth century BC. Identical animals and scenes are displayed on them, with certain minor differences that should not be ignored. There is no doubt however that the Romanian cups and the Rogozen cup deal with the same theme. An examination and comparison of them would help us to identify the common features of the Thracian pieces discovered in the two Danubian countries. Two of the Romanian cups were discovered at Agighiol in Dobrudzha. The third came from the Iron Gates on the Danube and is now in The Metropolitan Museum of Art, New York. That identical manufacturing techniques were used on the cups found in Romania and on the Rogozen cup is immediately obvious, while certain differences in composition do not affect their stylistic unity. These distinctions merely demonstrate that the four cups were made by different craftsmen: for example, the bird of prey clutching a fish and a hare is missing from the second Agighiol cup. In the tondo on the base of the Rogozen cup there is a wolf biting a boar, while on both the Metropolitan Museum cup and the first Agighiol cup, the boar is being attacked by a horned lion-griffin, which is not actually biting its prey but is clutching the leg of some other animal in its mouth.

The scenes on the Rogozen cup also have parallels on two silver helmets found in Romania. One of these is at present in the Detroit Arts Museum and the other is in the Bucharest Museum. A fish held in the beak of a bird of prey appears again, and when we add the image of a bird pecking a snake on a Rogozen jug (No. 162), the pattern becomes even more complete. It is known that the Thracians were illiterate and that their mythology was recorded in pictures rather than written texts. We already knew of representations of their deities on several works of art but the Rogozen treasure increases the number considerably. It is now necessary to identify all the images that appear and explain their significance: this will make a significant contribution to scholarship.

The Rogozen treasure, which brings to our attention new pictorial evidence, is an important find. I suggest that the entire series of images and scenes is in some way connected with the two major Thracian deities – the Great Goddess and the Divine Horseman – as they were known to and illustrated by the Thracians in the fifth and fourth centuries BC.

Bogdan Nikolov
Senior Research Associate

The Thracians and their Religion

Although a dazzling surprise to us, it would not at all have astonished the ancient Greeks that this huge treasure of silver and silver-gilt plate should be found in Thrace, especially in southern Thrace, the territory between the north Aegean and the Danube, most of which is now Bulgaria. They were well accustomed to the demands of the Thracian kings. According to Thucydides, Seuthes, who reigned from 424–410 BC and was admittedly one of the most rapacious, received from Thracian subordinates and the Greek colonies settled on his territory an annual tribute which amounted to about four hundred talents in gold and silver, equivalent in value to more than ten tons of silver, and the same again in the form of presents of artefacts made of precious metals. What is truly amazing is that such a collection of silver jugs and bowls has survived more than two thousand years to be discovered in our time by a man digging his garden.

Most important, of course, is what this new discovery can reveal about that enigmatic people, the Thracians, whom even their neighbours the Greeks, who mocked at their boorishness but were awed by their mysteries, never really fathomed.

The Thracians, Herodotos observed, were an exceptionally numerous people who, but for their chronic inability to unite, would in his opinion have been the most powerful of all nations. Their lands stretched northwards from the Aegean to the north Carpathian foothills. In present-day terms this includes northern Greece, Turkish Thrace and both shores of the Propontis (the Sea of Marmara), Bulgaria, Romania and much of Slovakia. Eastwards, where in the sixth century BC they came under the rule of the Scyths, they reached across Moldavia into the Ukrainian steppes to beyond the valley of the Dnieper. West of this vast area lay Hallstattian Central Europe where Celtic power was fermenting prior to its eruption south and east in the fourth and third centuries BC. South of this group were the Illyrians, whose border with Thracian tribes is difficult to distinguish. South of Illyria were the Macedonians, later to be a world power, and still further south the Greeks, whose expanding and culturally explosive cities extended also along the coast of western Asia Minor.

It is South Thrace, that part of the Thracian territories lying south of the Danube, with which we are chiefly concerned here. The Greeks saw it as a cold land, the kingdom of Boreas, the terrible north wind. In what is now Turkish Thrace Xenophon complained of the 'deep snow, so cold . . . the wine froze in the pots', while the Roman exile Ovid later noted that in the Dobroudja 'the snow lies deep and as it lies neither sun nor rains melt it . . . when the former ice has not yet melted, fresh succeeds'.

If the winters were cold, summers were probably hot and in the milder south such trees as the olive and bay and also the vine grew. The mountain ranges and a great part of the uplands were covered with permanent woods, both evergreen and deciduous. Wild animals were abundant and varied. They included wild bulls, bison, wolves, bears, wild boar, deer, hares and rabbits; in the south, according to legend, there were also lions and panthers. So the wild beasts on some of the Rogozen jugs would probably have been familar to local silversmiths. Rivers contained more water than they do now and were more navigable; they were also rich in fish.

Fighting and brigandage were their preferred occupations but the Thracians were also hunters, fishermen and farmers, with most of the work done by the women. They raised cattle, goats, pigs and horses, the last highly prized by the Greeks. So were the gold and silver mined on the island of Thasos and on Mount Pangaeus, timber for shipbuilding, obtained especially from the Strymon (Struma) valley, and the slaves which were essential for the underpinning of Greek democracy.

Polygamy was common among the Thracians. The favourite wives of chiefs and other nobles had the envied distinction of being ceremonially killed and buried with their husbands. Believing in an immortal and blessed afterlife, the Thracians had little fear of death.

The hard daily round was relieved by feasting, especially drinking. Unlike the Greeks, who mixed their wine with water, the Thracians drank theirs undiluted, often in one draught. This governed the type of bowl or goblet from which they found it convenient to drink. The silver bowls which are such an important feature of the Rogozen treasure must for the wealthy minority have replaced ones of clay, horn or wood as Persian and Greek imports increased in the fifth and fourth centuries.

The central *omphalos* or boss in some of the silver bowls was a convenient place for the second and third fingers when using these *phialae* for libations to the gods, as was their original purpose. Macrobius quotes Aristotle as saying that in one sanctuary of Dionysos in Thrace the priest made prophecies after drinking much pure wine. The Rogozen treasure could have been acquired and used for religious as well as secular purposes.

Thracian emergence from the darkness of prehistory into the then modern world began with the activities of Greek settlers in the eighth and seventh centuries BC. Slowly and hesitantly, Greek pioneers founded colonies on the coasts of the north Aegean, the Propontis and the Black Sea. At first, with Asia Minor ceasing to be a land of opportunity, their primary purpose was the acquisition of territory to which to emigrate. Conflict with the local Thracian tribes was inevitable. Homer's description of an incident of the Trojan War could well have been an account of another a few centuries later: Peiros, a Thracian captain, having smashed the ankle of Greek Diores with a stone, killed him with his spear. Then Aetolian Thoas thrust his spear into Peiros' chest, pulled the heavy weapon away and, 'drawing his sharp sword, struck him full in the belly. He took Peiros' life but did not get his armour. For Peiros' men, the Thracians with the topknots on their heads, surrounded him. They held their long spears steady in their hands and fended Thoas off, big, strong and formidable though he was. Thoas was shaken and withdrew' (trans. E. V. Rieu). The first Greeks who tried to settle Abdera on the north Aegean coast towards the middle of the seventh century were also obliged to withdraw; Abdera did not become a Greek colony for another hundred years or more.

The sixth century saw the Greeks increasingly developing their trading operations, on which the prosperity of their parent cities in Greece and Asia Minor now largely depended. This trade suffered a severe although not complete setback when, in about 513 BC, Darius with a huge Persian army crossed the Propontis and marched north to the Danube, accepting the submission of the Thracian tribes as he went. Generally the Persians seem to have been welcomed; only the Getai tribe in the lower Danube area resisted, thereby earning Herodotos' eulogy that they were the most just and valiant of the Thracians. Darius' primary intention was to attack the Scythian nomads in the Ukrainian steppe, operations against their eastern flank having proved abortive. Although equally unsuccessful in the west, he created a satrapy in Thrace from which to operate against Greece. The satrapy lasted for thirty-five years but some degree of Persian presence was maintained at least in Aegean Thrace until 465 BC.

Only Greek sources, incomplete and necessarily biased, exist to give an idea of this period, but subjugation under a great centralised state, in which the will of the monarch was universal law and whose power and wealth was beyond the imagination of his Thracian subjects, must have been an extraordinary and profound experience for a people who had previously only known their own primitive way of life. Roads were constructed, garrisons established at strategic points and the satrapy, regardless of tribal divisions, was ruled as a single unit.

The Odrysian tribe, originally centred on the south-east, had not opposed the Persian advance. Under the satrapy they prospered and gained an education in political leadership which came to fruition when the Persians departed. They, and others later, adopted from the Persians the pectoral as an insignia of rank. This was a gold plaque, variously decorated, worn on the breast in life and buried with the wearer, together with other possessions of value.

The lavish gifts made by the Persians to those who supported and rendered them service must also have made a deep impression. Xenophon relates that a suitable present to an ally was a horse with a gold bit, a gold necklet and armlets, a gold sword and a Persian robe. In the Odrysian royal cemetery at Douvanli, near Plovdiv, a silver-gilt amphora of fine Achaemenid workmanship was probably one of the gifts marking Persian-Odrysian friendship. A few *phialae* or bowls of the Rogozen treasure, worked in the Achaemenid style and probably from workshops situated in western Asia, may perhaps have come to Thrace at about this time. Two closely similar examples to one of the bowls (No. 2) have been found in Macedonia, one from a grave at Sindos dated 510–500 BC, the other from a grave dated to the first half of the fifth century at Kozani. Some of the plainer Rogozen bowls also have Achaemenid shapes but, as D. E. Strong observed, 'In the Hellenistic period there was a complicated interaction of Greek and Achaemenid forms of *phiale* upon one another and there are many problems connected with the various forms which still remain to be solved'. Written in 1966, this is still true, but the Rogozen treasure will provide a unique contribution to specialist study of such objects.

The Thracians did not depend entirely on presents to build up their collections of valuables. Boges, commander of the Persian garrison at the mouth of the Strymon, was besieged by a Greek army and faced starvation. Rather than surrender he slew his wife, children, concubines and servants, threw his treasure of gold and silver into the river, and then committed suicide. Whether the treasure ended up in Thracian or Greek hands is not known. Herodotos is also vague regarding the fate of the Persian 'sacred chariot'. In the order of march of the Persian army this was preceded by ten magnificently harnessed sacred white horses. Behind these the chariot was drawn by eight more white horses, its charioteer walking behind, since no mortal man might ride it. The royal chariot with Xerxes followed. Herodotos refers to the former as the sacred chariot of Zeus, but to the Persians it was probably a central part of a solar cult. When Xerxes invaded Greece in 480 BC he left it in the care of the Paeonian tribe in the Strymon valley. On his return it was missing. The Paeonians who, according to Herodotos, had given it to the Thracians, complained that the mares (and presumably the chariot) had been stolen by Thracians.

The final withdrawal of Persia from South Thrace, in about 465, left an apparent power vacuum which Athens was unable to fill. The Scyths saw it as their opportunity to extend their dominions to the Aegean. Already in 496 they had raided as far south as the Gallipoli peninsula. But it was the Persian-fostered Odrysians who seized the opportunity. Their king Teres – of whom Plutarch wrote that when not fighting he strove to be indistinguishable from his grooms – was able to raise an army of sufficient strength in time to meet the Scyths on the Danube and conclude an amicable peace treaty.

Sitalkes, Teres' successor (431–24), extended his power far beyond the old Odrysian tribal territory and loosely controlled an area probably extending from the Danube delta to the vicinity of Byzantion (Istanbul) and westward as far as the Strymon and Oescus (Iskur) rivers. A genuine philhellene, whose son was given Athenian citizenship, he at once established diplomatic relations with Athens which sought Thracian help against the rising power of Macedonia. Sitalkes invaded his western neighbour with an army which, swollen by followers seeking loot, was said to number 150,000. It may have been this exploit that figured in the ballad of Sitalkes, which Xenophon heard sung in Paphlagonia by a Thracian after a banquet at which he and his fellows had danced dressed in full armour to a flute. The invasion foundered through lack of promised Athenian support. In broad commercial terms the alliance was more fruitful for the Thracians, whose appetite for gifts had been whetted by the munificence of the Persians. 'It was impossible to accomplish anything without making gifts', complained Thucydides. Luxury imports of pottery, silver plate, bronze vessels and sometimes gold jewellery followed those from Persia. Greek exports included artefacts in oriental style or with oriental elements to please those who had developed a taste for them, a fact which needs to be remembered in looking at the Rogozen treasure.

Sitalkes was assassinated in 424 in the course of an expedition against the Triballi, the Thracian tribe west of the Iskur whose lands stretched to the Nishava and Morava rivers. The Triballi, like the Bessi tribe in the Rhodope region, were especially noted for their fighting qualities and, although they were driven from Serbia by the Celts and were constantly forced into periods of temporary submission, they were probably never really conquered until the arrival of the Romans. It is in Triballi country, halfway between the modern town of Vratsa and the Danube, that the Rogozen treasure was found. In Vratsa itself in a tumulus containing three royal graves, at Bukyovtsi by the Danube and at Alexandrovo, Radyuvene, Loukovit and Letnitsa in the nearby district of Lovech, rich if smaller finds include silver vessels, some with similar or related forms and some bearing similar inscriptions. They are testimony to Triballi wealth as well as to this tribe's turbulent history.

With the death of Sitalkes a period of decline and disintegration set in for the Odrysian kingdom. Only one king, Kotys, who ruled from 384–3 to 359, was successful in halting its progress. Described by the Greeks as a fierce and evil man, a skilful and treacherous diplomat, he was also notorious for his propensity for banquets, and an Attic comedy made fun of the one he offered for the wedding of his daughter to the Athenian Iphicrates. Athenaeus repeats scurrilous tales told of Kotys by Theopompus, but also records a visit later paid by Philip of Macedon to Onocarsis, an estate of Kotys in Thrace, 'which included a beautifully planted grove and one well adapted for a pleasant sojourn especially in the summer season. In fact it had been one of the favorite resorts of Kotys, who, more than any other king that had arisen in Thrace, directed his career towards the enjoyment of pleasures and luxuries. As he went about the country, wherever he discovered places shaded with trees and watered with running streams, he turned them into banqueting places. Visiting each in turn, as chance led him, he would offer sacrifices to the gods and hold court with his lieutenants' (trans. after C. B. Gulick). Kotys is not an unusual Thracian name, especially among the Odrysai, but it has been suggested that it was this Kotys whose name is inscribed on some of the silver vessels at Rogozen, as well as on others discovered elsewhere in Thrace, and it would be pleasantly appropriate if this proved so. Kotys' reign was not peaceful and during it, in 379, the Triballi came south on a marauding expedition as far as Abdera, which was only relieved with Athenian help. Such an excursion must have resulted in much rich booty.

The year of Kotys' death saw the accession to the throne of Macedonia of Philip II, who quickly moved against Thrace as part of his grand design. Philip, who claimed descent from Herakles and to whom the saying is attributed that there was no fortress he could not capture with one donkey laden with gold, soon obtained possession of and began to exploit the mines of Pangaeus. Gradually he brought under his control Kersebleptes, Kotys' son and successor – another name inscribed on a Rogozen vessel – and other princes, and by 341 had established himself as ruler of South Thrace although the effectiveness of his dominion north of the Balkan range is to be doubted.

Macedonian colonies were now established for the first time in the interior. They included Philippopolis (modern Plovdiv) on the Hebros (Maritsa). Although the Athenians made fun of these settlements, they must have played a considerable part in the diffusion of Greek and Macedonian culture and technical skills to the Thracians.

In 336 Philip was succeeded by Alexander, who in the following year crossed the Balkan range, defeated the Triballi, put fear into the Getai and for the time being quietened the whole region. He is also said to have met a delegation of Celts while on the Danube. In 334 Alexander crossed the Hellespont to begin his conquest of the known world and beyond. His army included Thracian cavalry and infantry units, each under a tribal leader from, *inter alia*, the Odrysai and the Triballi. Throughout written history Thracians were renowned as fighters, whether for freedom, booty or pay, and as gladiators under the Roman Empire. It has been suggested that they were the original peltasts, infantry with a light shield and two spears for throwing or else one heavy one for thrusting and a short sword. This could perhaps explain an otherwise mysterious third spear in the scene of a boar hunt on one of the Rogozen jugs (No. 159) where both hunters, admittedly on horseback, are each still in possession of a spear.

Although weakened by the loss of their best fighters to Alexander's army, Thracian leaders naturally took advantage of his absence and the confusion following his death. His successor in Thrace, Lysimachos, who was as greedy for tribute as any Thracian king and drove some of the West Pontic Greek cities into alliances with the Thracians, finally succeeded in restoring and maintaining order. In the course of his campaigns, Lysimachos was captured by the Getai and diplomatically released. During the temporary period of peace which he established, an Odrysian king – Seuthes III – achieved a small Hellenistic-style capital far up the Tonzos (Tundja) valley. The excavations here of thirty years ago unearthed no treasure of precious metal – Seuthopolis had been sacked and put to the flames by the Celts – but there were remains of a palace, houses, streets, fortifications, and plenty of wheel-made ware, both imported and locally made, as well as Thracian coinage to show the newly developing Thracian polity. This ended when the death of Lysimachos in 281 gave the Celts their chance for a massive invasion of the Balkan peninsula. One prong of their attack was directed against the Triballi, already driven from parts of their earlier territories, whilst another succeeded in establishing a kingdom in the original homeland of the Odrysai which lasted for sixty years.

Contact between Greeks and the South Thracians had existed during the Late Bronze Age. Although this contact had ended with the fall of Mycenaean Greece, its memory persisted in orally-transmitted Greek legends, some of which eventually became enshrined in literature. During the Trojan War Thracian tribes were among Troy's allies, perhaps reflecting a common effort to halt Mycenaean expansion into the Thracian interior and the Black Sea. An episode in the *Iliad* tells us of the Thracian king Rhesus, whose magnificent gold armour was said to be fit only for gods to wear. He was slain while asleep in a night raid by Diomedes, who stole his famous white horses with the help of Odysseus. Three Thracians, Orpheus and two sons of Boreas, are listed among the Argonauts. Boreas, the North Wind, blew from Thrace. He abducted Oreithyia, the daughter of Erechtheus, king of Athens, and took her to Thrace.

Orpheus, the son of the Thracian king Oiagros and the muse Kalliope, is the hero of Graeco-Thracian legend who exerted most influence on later Greek thought. Because he refused to worship Dionysos, but every morning climbed Mount Pangaeus to greet the sun god Apollo, Dionysos roused the Thracian women to kill him. The ancient Greeks considered Orpheus to be a religious reformer and an inspired teacher, and Orphism exerted a profound influence on Greek philosophy and religion. Dionysos, who represented the orgiastic side of religion in opposition to Orphism, was also the god of vegetation and was reputed to have brought the vine from Thrace to Greece.

From these and other legends Thracian impact on Greece in the early period can be registered, even if the means are mythological rather than factual. Of the corresponding impact of Greece on Thrace we have no information whatsoever. The Thracians never committed their language, which belonged to the Indo-European group, to writing. The short inscriptions appearing on several of the bowls and two of the jugs belonging to the Rogozen treasure are written in Greek letters, but represent Thracian names of persons and, sometimes, places.

One longer Thracian inscription, using some sixty Greek letters, appears on the bezel of a gold finger-ring from Ezerovo in Central Bulgaria. Another, more obscure but about the same length, appears on a stone slab near Preslav in north-eastern Bulgaria and there are two fragmentary inscriptions from a sanctuary on Samothrace. These are the only known examples of written Thracian that are longer than the Rogozen type of inscription and, despite numerous attempts, none has been satisfactorily deciphered.

After Philip of Macedon's conquest of South Thrace in the mid-fourth century, whether under direct Macedonian or Thracian rule, Greek served for all official purposes, including treaties and decrees, and remained the *lingua franca* of the eastern and southern areas. When Rome absorbed South Thrace into her empire in the first century AD, Latin tended to replace Greek in the more heavily Romanised regions, as it did north of the Danube after the conquest of Dacia, comprising modern Oltenia and Transylvania. Although Thracian must have continued as a spoken language, when the ethnic identity of the Thracian peoples was gradually broken up in the turmoil of the ending of the Roman empire and the wave of migrations that was both a cause and a consequence, the Thracian language still remained unwritten. Unfortunately, the use of Greek and Latin by Thracians did not extend to recording their own religion or mythology.

The Thracian disinclination to commit their religion, mythology and traditions to writing was not an uncommon trait. Brahmanic tradition so opposed such desecration of their holy word that it was only recorded, at the instigation of foreign scholars, in the late eighteenth and early nineteenth centuries. Among the Gauls, Caesar comments that Druidic principles similarly opposed any recording of their religion. In Mycenaean Greece, Linear B tablets provide us with no theological texts, hymns or temple dedications. Names of gods occur, but only as recipients of stores issued by palace administrators, and without mention of divine attributes or rituals. These analogies suggest that the oral traditions governing Thracian religion may likewise have exercised a taboo on the admission of strangers to their holy secrets, a prohibition which writing about them either in Thracian or any other language would have broken.

Consequently archaeology remains our only Thracian source for the elucidation of Thracian religion. Unfortunately, archaeology's reliance upon the illogicalities of survival and discovery means that its evidence is often capable of more than one interpretation. Although it can be supplemented by the writings of Greek and Latin authors, these looked at Thrace through usually biased Greek or Roman eyes. Even the judgment of that admirable and conscientious observer Herodotos, who visited South Thrace probably towards the end of the first half of the fifth century, could not but be affected by his Greek background. Moreover, since he had no first-hand knowledge of the Thracian interior, he was obliged to rely for information on the accounts of travellers whose perspicacity and discrimination varied considerably.

Had Herodotos possessed a deeper knowledge of the Thracians, he might well have compared them with the Achaemenid Persians, of whom he wrote that it was not their custom to erect statues, temples or altars – and that they considered anyone a fool who did so – since the Persian religion is not anthropomorphic like the Greek. They climb, he continued, to the mountain-tops and sacrifice to Zeus who, to them, is the whole circle of the heavens; they worship the sun, the moon, the earth, fire, water and the winds. Archaeology is providing increasing evidence for an ancient Thracian religion that closely resembled this description of the Persian. Before the impact of Greece the Thracians did not build temples, nor is there any evidence for anthropomorphic gods; this concept was a Greek contribution, and we cannot be certain that it was ever accepted into Thracian religion. Mountain peaks may have been especially important places for worship, but other natural features such as springs and caves were also cult centres. Many of these emerged into history in the Hellenistic period, continued into the Roman, were adopted by the Slavs in the sixth and seventh centuries and

in some cases became places of pilgrimage under Christianity.

Bronze Age potsherds found on the Rhodope peak of G'oz-tepe, claimed by the Greeks in Hellenistic times to be a shrine of Dionysos, suggest that this was earlier a sacred spot. Other evidence of the solar cult has been found in the Sakar hills of south-east Bulgaria, where high rocks have been carved with discs so cut that their mica surfaces catch the first gleams of the rising sun. Specially-cut niches in other mountainous parts are similarly oriented. On pottery this cult is reflected in the running spiral decoration of the Middle Bronze Age and the tangential circles of the Early Iron Age. A ritual deposit of the tenth to eighth centuries BC excavated in the city of Sofia, included a gold bowl with tangential circles decorating its base. This ornament occurs in precisely similar fashion on the bases of three of the Rogozen bowls and beneath the animals' hooves on the goblet (No. 165), as well as on the handles of two of the jugs. It also decorates a Thracian bridle frontal bearing a miniature horse's head from a contemporary burial at Oguz in the eastern Ukraine. This solar cult is also reflected in the whirling sun disc on a silver rhyton from Poroina in Oltenia and on five bull-head bridle plaques belonging to the Craiova treasure from the same region. In this form it appears in the Rogozen treasure on the *phiale* with the six bulls' heads, their forelocks curving from a central disc to produce a sense of movement (No. 94).

Farther north in Transylvania, where the Dacian tribes who had assimilated a major Celtic influx in the third century BC were facing the might of Rome, great circular and rectangular sanctuaries open to the sky enshrined their urano-solar cults. Little is known of the rites for which the sanctuaries were constructed, but the Roman conquest was not considered to have been completed until these temples had been razed to the ground. Herodotos makes no specific mention of a Thracian solar cult, but he describes the habit of the Getai of shooting arrows towards the sky during thunderstorms to scare away the foreign god who was threatening their own.

Syncretism of sun and hearth cults can be traced in the Middle Bronze Age hearth discovered at Sighişoara, formerly Wietenberg, in

Transylvania. It is edged with the solar symbol of the running spiral. The same motif appears almost identically on seventh-century BC Thracian hearth altars at Zhabotin on a tributary of the Dnieper, and at Bosut Gradina in northern Serbia. It is found again in a Thracian settlement just north of the Danube at Popeşti, in Muntenia, in a relatively large building of the second century BC. Variously decorated hearth altars appear elsewhere in Thracian-occupied parts of the Ukraine, and are a feature of Seuthopolis where, usually with vegetal and geometric decoration, they occur in each dwelling as well as in the sanctuary of the Great Samothracian Gods and in the palace throne room. Another aspect of the syncretic cult of which the hearth was a focal point occurs in the enigmatic Late Bronze Age *zolniki* of the Noua culture in Moldavia. These were mounds constructed largely of ashes from hearths, fragmented pieces of hearths and stoves, broken pots and tools and animal bones. Sometimes they contained whole hearths or even whole dwellings. The hearth was a sacred symbol of the continuity of existence of family life from generation to generation and was thus linked with ancestral cults, just as its life-sustaining fire and heat linked it with those of the sun.

The Indo-European ancestry of the Thracians dates from the arrival of the migrants from the steppes at the beginning of the Early Bronze Age, bringing with them a cult of the horned animal. This cult, in the form of either bulls' or rams' heads or simply as symbolic representations of horns, persisted among the Thracians until they ceased to exist as an ethnic entity. In the Rogozen treasure we have evidence of it on the bowl (No. 94) with the sun symbols on the bull heads and in the ram head frieze on a jug (No. 162), where it may indicate kingship over the mythological and real animal worlds.

From the Early Bronze Age onwards Thrace had been culturally isolated from the emergent civilisations of western Asia. Unlike the Greeks, the evolution of whose religion and mythology reflected their geographical openness to such influences, the Thracians retained in primitive form those basic tenets of Indo-European religion which are so vividly described with zoomorphic and anthropomorphic imagery in the *Rig Veda*. Consequently Thracian syncretism of cults of the

sun, of fire, of the hearth, of ancestors and of the horned animal are in essence the same as those in the *Rig Veda* hymns. How they were represented in Thracian oral tradition, unfortunately, we cannot know, but in the Rogozen treasure we may perhaps gain glimpses of them.

In the Vedic hymns we find Surya, the sun, represented as a horse, as a winged horse, as a chariot drawn by white horses, as an eagle, or simply as a wheel; Indra, the king of gods, as a horse, a bull, a ram or a goat. An expression of concepts representing the sun in Thracian art appears on a small gold jug from a rich fourth-century husband and wife burial at Vratsa, only twenty-eight miles from Rogozen. On the body of the jug two identical male figures, each seated in winged chariots, are driving quadrigae (*Fig.* 1). The duality of the scene as well as its substance finds a reflection in Vedic imagery of Surya and more examples of this appear in the Rogozen treasure.

A jug (No. 157) of the Rogozen treasure displays two quadrigae of winged horses drawing chariots in which again male or female persons of clear importance are seated. In the boar hunt scene on another jug (No. 159) the two hunters are mounted on horses. A round *phalera* from another important treasure found at Letnitsa, also in north-east Bulgaria, has eight bridled horseheads encircling a central boss. The Indo-European principle of *pars pro toto* meant that a horse head could mean not only a whole horse but many horses, and it was also part of solar imagery. The riding and chariot horses of kings and chiefs were usually buried with them, sometimes the chariots as well. Silver plaques that decorated their horses' bridles often consisted of three or four heads of horses, bears or mythological animals such as griffins in profile round a central boss to form a swastika-like tetraskele or triskele sun symbol (*Fig.* 2).

The scene of a lion attacking a doe, which appears on two Rogozen jugs (Nos. 155, 156), and also on the base of the goblet (No. 165) where a wolf is attacking a boar, are versions of the theme of an animal with claws overpowering one with hooves, a popular motif in Thracian iconography. Two silver plaques in the Loukovit treasure show a lion attacking a stag. In the centre of a silver dish from a hoard discovered at Borovo,

Fig. 1   Gold jug, Vratsa *(Photo R. Staneva)*

near Rousse, a griffin is shown descending on a stag. On a Vratsa bridle plaque a lion attacks a deer (*Fig.* 3). Two Letnitsa belt plaques carry other versions of the same theme; on one there is a wolf and a doe, on the other a griffin and an elk. The dualistic concept of cosmic order and chaos, the former also represented on earth by a king as the earthly incarnation of deity, was Indo-Iranian. Its expression in animal art had been early adopted

Fig. 2   Silver bridle plaque, Loukovit *(Photo R. Staneva)*

Fig. 3   Silver bridle plaque, Vratsa *(Photo R. Staneva)*

by the Scyths, whence it came to the Thracians for whom it must have expressed similar concepts.

A different predatory theme appears on the side of the Rogozen goblet (No. 165). Here the predator is a huge unicorn bird with a fish in its beak and an immense claw with which it grasps its victim, a hare. The unicorn bird may represent deity with power over land and water. The goblet is very closely related to three others. Two of them, one from a burial at Agighiol in the Romanian Dobroudja, (*Fig.* 4) the other now in New York, carry the identical scene, which is again repeated on the cheekpieces of two helmets found north of the Danube, one at Peretu in Muntenia, the other near the Danubian Iron Gates and now in Detroit. It is possible that this ´group, stylistically completely different from anything else at Rogozen, was Getic work and that the Rogozen goblet was either booty from a Triballi raid or an inter-tribal gift.

The concept of divine kingship is also indicated on two of the bowls. On one (No. 96), with a griffin at the base, a frieze of eagles alternates with palmettes. On the other (No. 98), eight highly stylised eagles' heads encircle the central boss. The sun symbols on a bowl (No. 94) have already been mentioned (p. 27). In Vedic terms they would represent a syncretism of the cults of Indra and Surya.

In the *Rig Veda*, Yama, king of the dead, was the first mortal to reach the other world and the pathfinder for his fellows. He was the first ancestor and the hymn in his honour calls upon him and others, the 'fathers' now with him, to aid those

Fig. 4   Silver goblet, Agighiol *(Photo British Museum)*

still to come. This concept of an ancestor who from the afterlife would assist his followers to join him was as fervently held by the Thracians. A proof of this can be found in the Hero – a religious concept shared by Thracians and Greeks, both with Indo-European roots. Attaining immortality through superhuman deeds, the Hero had the power to help those still on earth.

Although rejecting literacy, by the fourth century the Thracians felt able to accept, within the limitations imposed by their non-anthropomorphic concept of deity, the, to them, new idea of representational art. It is significant that the first and most popular personage borrowed from Greek religion was Herakles, a hero who had achieved divinity through his heroic labours on earth. Naively depicted, holding his club, the other hand resting on a minute Nemean lion, Herakles is shown on a silver plaque from a fourth century BC tumulus burial at Panagyurishte, and from the same place a probably later *phalera* shows the same episode. Herakles appears twice in the Rogozen treasure. The *phiale* with Herakles and the priestess Auge (No. 4) is a straight copy of a Greek theme, even to the nakedness of the two figures which was not at all in accordance with Thracian principles. Auge is correctly named; but the Hero's name is not Herakles but Delade. Can this have been a sycophantic act on the craftsman's part, insinuat-

ing that his patron is another Herakles? The other Rogozen example is the Amazon scene on a jug (No. 154). Here the craftsman chooses only to illustrate, three times, an Amazon attacking Herakles with a spear. In the background, between the figures, are three bears standing on their hind legs and two heads of horses. The bears may indicate the wildness of the Amazon country, the horseheads, on the *pars pro toto* principle, the Amazons' great wealth by virtue of their large herds of horses.

But Thracians also depicted their own Hero. It is he who appears in dual form on the Vratsa jug (Fig. 1) and he and a female counterpart ride in the quadrigae of the Rogozen jug (No. 157). The fullest expression of the Thracian Chieftain – Hero concept appears on a series of silver belt plaques. They were found, like the horsehead *phalera* but the work of a different craftsman, in the Letnitsa hoard. Except in the final scene the Hero is mounted. One plaque shows him as a great hunter, spearing a bear, a dead wolf lying between his horse's hooves. On another he holds a spear, while behind his back a bow occupies a vacant corner of the rectangular plaque; it symbolises his prowess in battle and his mastery of weapons (*Fig. 5*). On two of the plaques a man's head and on another a woman's occupy the same vacant spaces, showing him to be chief of a large tribe (*Fig. 6*), and on one more a horse's head proclaims his wealth and perhaps the blessing of the sun (*Fig. 7*). Another has two possible interpretations. He holds a *phiale* for wine instead of a spear and behind him is an animal which may represent his power over the animal world (*Fig. 8*). Alternatively, in terms used by the Vedic hymnists, his *phiale* may contain *soma*, the ambrosial drink which confers immortality, and the animal may be his dog Saramā, the bitch of Indra, whose two offspring guard the entrance to the heavenly afterlife. These may not, of course, be alternatives; it may be intended that elements of both are to be read into the scene. To the Thracians, both feasting and hunting, and particularly the boar hunt although this is not shown in the Letnitsa plaques, had important religious undertones. A final scene in this series, unless the last-mentioned was so intended, shows the return of the hero to his wife and home, where he fulfils his ancestral role of fathering his tribe. Behind the pair a

Fig. 5   Silver belt plaque, Letnitsa *(Photo S. Boyadjiev)*

Fig. 6   Silver belt plaque, Letnitsa *(Photo S. Boyadjiev)*

Fig. 7   Silver belt plaque, Letnitsa *(Photo S. Boyadjiev)*

Fig. 8   Silver belt plaque, Letnitsa *(Photo S. Boyadjiev)*

woman holds a jug of wine, the vessel very similar to several in the Rogozen treasure, and waves a branch between them (*Fig. 11*).

Such a Chieftain – Hero recalls Rhesus, of whom Thracian legends were still extant in the first half of the third century AD when Philostratos wrote: 'Rhesus, whom Diomedes slew at Troy, is said to inhabit Rhodope, and they recount many wondrous deeds of his; for they say that he breeds horses and marches in armour, and hunts wild beasts; and, in proof that the hero is a hunter, they tell how the wild boar and gazelles and all the beasts of the mountain come by twos and threes to the altar of Rhesus, and are offered in sacrifice, unbound and unfettered, and yield themselves to the knife; and this hero is said to ward off plague

from his borders' (trans. W. H. Porter). More than two thousand stone tablets of the mounted Thracian Hero, usually portrayed as a hunter with his dog, and often in the act of spearing a boar issuing from behind a serpent-entwined tree, have been discovered in Bulgaria and neighbouring countries. The majority are dated to the second or third centuries AD. Some of them have been found where they had even been absorbed into Christianity as icons of St George.

Except for the jug on which two horsemen are hunting a boar, the mounted Hero does not appear in the Rogozen treasure. One jug, however (No. 158), has a centrally-placed winged figure, which I take to be a man, who is holding two dogs. On either side of them are two winged horses

Fig. 9   Silver rhyton, Poroina *(Photo CPCS Bucarest)*

with male human heads. Beneath him a bull crouches as it is about to be attacked by four dogs. This is not Greek iconography and were the winged figure intended to be female it is closer to Lilith, the Sumerian goddess of death, than to Artemis. In Vedic terms the central figure is Yama, king of the dead, with his two guardian dogs which are killers but also guides who show the dead the path to heaven. Mythological beasts in attendance show Yama's situation at the gates of the afterlife, while below a bull is about to meet the death which must precede immortality.

These Indo-European concepts which the Rogozen treasure illustrates so vividly offer a wide new interpretation of Thracian art, one which needs to be explored with great care for, as has been pointed out, archaeology may often be interpreted in more than one way. It is a challenge, perhaps an impossible one, facing archaeology or anthropology to trace how such concepts can have persisted orally for some three millennia. They may have been stimulated but cannot have been created by the shortlived Persian occupation.

Another feature of the Rogozen treasure is the prominence given to female figures. Hitherto we have only encountered this aspect of Thracian religion on the Poroina *rhyton* (Fig. 9). There, a scene of a seated woman holding a *rhyton* and a bowl and attended by another standing behind her is shown twice, another example of Indo-European duality. It should be considered together with those on two Rogozen jugs, one where two women ride lionesses on either side of the lion-stag combat (No. 155), the second where a woman seated in one of the two chariots drawn by winged quadrigae is opposed by a man holding a bow in the other (No. 157). That the female principle, whether primarily considered as expressing nature, fertility or intercession with heavenly powers, must have been of cardinal importance in Thracian religion is shown by the adoption of Bendis, a Thracian 'goddess', into the official pantheon of Athens.

The name of Bendis, and since the Bithynian Thracians called one of their months the Bendidos a corresponding cult is assumed, first occurs in the writings of the Ionian sixth century BC poet Hipponax. In the second half of the fifth century, clear literary and epigraphic evidence for a Bendis

cult appears in Athens where it existed among the large numbers of Hellenised Thracians living there, mostly as a consequence of the slave trade. In 431 the Peloponnesians invaded Attica and were ravaging the countryside. The Athenians, their control of Delphi lost, were obliged to resort to the oracle of Zeus at Dodona in Epirus. The oracle appears to have recommended that the Thracian population be permitted a shrine. As other evidence suggests that they already had one, perhaps it was intended that it should have more official support. It was about this time that an alliance with the Thracian king Sitalkes was concluded and the oracle's answer may have had political overtones. In the following year a severe plague epidemic broke out in Athens and another delegation was sent to Dodona. This time the oracle replied that it was essential that Bendis be placated with an official cult, which would include the sacrifice of oxen, construction of a temple and a cult statue, and an annual festival with torchlight and horseback processions of which Plato has given us a lively account. This official cult did not last many years. Soon afterwards the cult of Asklepios was introduced to Athens and, Bendis being no longer required to cope with plague, her official cult was absorbed into that of

31

Fig. 10   4th-century Attic stele *(Photo British Museum)*

Artemis, although it persisted for much longer among the Thracian population. Bendis is represented on a fourth-century Attic stele now in the British Museum (*Fig. 10*). Dressed in a Thracian cap and tunic, animal-skin apron, short pleated skirt and high boots, she turns towards a line of torch-bearers.

It has been suggested that Bendis was a Great Mother – Goddess, but I think it more consonant with Thracian religion that she was a female counterpart of the Hero. The royal status of this person we have called Bendis is demonstrated on the jug (No. 155) where she appears twice, seated on a lioness, consort of the king of beasts. The importance of her fertility aspect appears in her portrayal, holding the bough, in the chariot drawn by a quadriga of winged horses (No. 157) and it must surely be the same person who appears with the bough on the Letnitsa plaque (*Fig. 11*). A gaily decorated 'wedding tree' or bough is a traditional accompaniment to some peasant marriage ceremonies in Bulgaria today. Possibly to the Thracians it was also Bendis who offers the dish of pomegranates to the Thracian noble and his wife in the tomb painting at Kazanluk, near excavated Seuthopolis.

Although we can be sure that the jug decorations with figural compositions are original Thracian work, some of the other jugs and some of the bowls, which form the majority of the treasure, may be imports or, in many cases, Thracian copies of imports. Only one jug is quite plain except for a band encircling its shoulder (No. 109); it compares with two others found in Bulgaria, one from Loukovit, the other from a burial at Vurbitsa, near Preslav. The lotus flower decoration (Nos. 143–153) also appears on a jug from Rozovets, near Plovdiv, on a particularly splendid example from the rich Derveni cemetery in Macedonia, where it is dated to the second half of the fourth century, and on another from Tell el-Maskhuta (ancient Pithom) in Egypt. The last, dated to the early fourth century, may indicate the origin of this type.

Isolated human heads, sometimes with a small part of the neck, are a common decorative feature in the Rogozen treasure; they also occur on jewellery from Boukyovtsi, on a bowl from Loukovit and on a *skyphos* from a tomb at Strelcha near Pazardjik. Leaving aside three of the Rogozen bowls (Nos. 101–103), clearly copied from such a model as the Aphrodite bowl from nearby Vratsa,

Catalogue No. 4

Catalogue No. 2

Catalogue No. 155

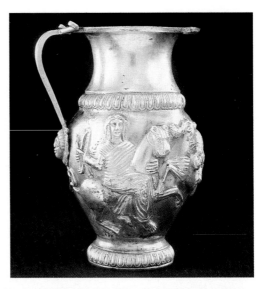

Catalogue No. 97

Catalogue No. 136

Catalogue No. 163

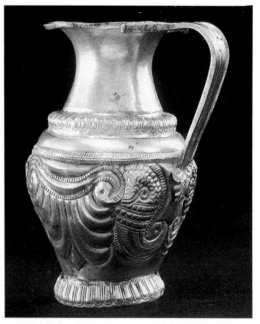

Catalogue No. 161

Catalogue No. 164

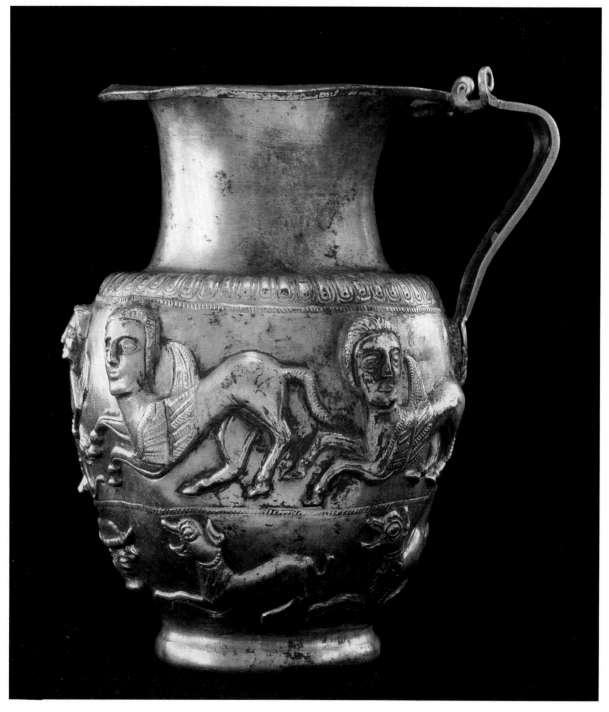

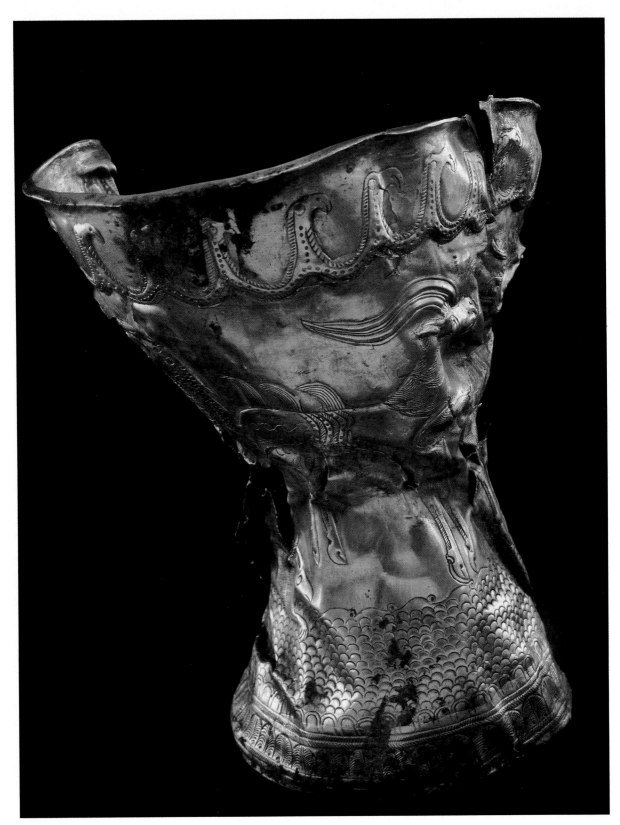

Catalogue No. 165

Fig. 11 Silver belt plaque, Letnitsa *(Photo S. Boyadjiev)*

there is a large head above the griffin on a jug (No. 162), and two smaller ones on handle bases (Nos. 155 and 159), the latter with another head below it. On two bowls, heads form the main decoration (eight on No. 99 and seven on No. 100), the latter being perhaps a clumsy imitation of the former. These heads could be symbolic representations of one or more persons, some even apotropaic symbols of the Hero or Bendis. But some, although not the head above the griffin, have a Celtic look and must be studied together with finds from Central Europe, such as the Hořovičky bronze *phalera*, in view of the proximity of the Celtic

Skordisci tribe to the Triballi. Thrace was a route between the Orient and the Celts, and is considered to be an intermediary through which Achaemenid influences passed to the latter. The upper zone of stags on the situla in Grave 6–7–7a and the lead horsehead tetraskele in Grave 31 from Tumulus V at Magdalenska Gora in Slovenia are two examples of Thracian influence on Celtic art.

I have suggested earlier the Rogozen treasure probably served for both religious and secular feasts. It may have belonged to a line of Triballi kings and thus have been accumulated over many years. Only one thing is certain; it did not come from a burial or its inventory would include such objects as horse harness and jewellery. The earliest pieces may date to the period of Persian occupation, but as the fashion for these continued long after the Persians' departure, much further study is needed on this and other dating problems of individual vessels. It is my tentative view that the treasure is likely to have been buried to avoid capture by the Celts invading Triballi territory in 279 BC. After that it would not have been safe to recover it for a long time, not until it and its hiding place had been forgotten. However there must have been other occasions in which the treasure could have been hastily concealed by a few people, whether its legitimate owners or robbers, who were eliminated before it could be recovered. By any reckoning, Rogozen is an exceptional find; the circumstances of both its accumulation and its concealment may be exceptional too.

R. F. Hoddinott

The Catalogue

1 Silver phiale
Diam. 19.6 cm; h. 4.8 cm
Inv. no. 22301
Rim cracked.
Around the boss are three rings of raised beading, arcs and a zig-zag line. The body is decorated with a band of broad radial fluting.

2 Silver-gilt phiale   *See colour plates*
Diam. 20.3 cm; h. 4.1 cm
Inv. no. 22302
Boss split; holes in the body.
The boss is encircled by a wide band of raised almond nuts arranged radially alternating with lotus blossoms. The decoration is convex on the outside.

1

3 Silver phiale
Max. diam. 18.1 cm; max. h. 4.0 cm
Inv. no. 22303
Crushed before discovery, with rim split in places.
Around the boss is a ring of acorns. The rest of the surface is decorated with a scale pattern resembling a fir-cone.

4 Silver-gilt phiale   *See colour plates*
Diam. 13.6 cm; h. 2.0 cm
Inv. no. 22304
The phiale has an inner disc, made separately with figures in relief and carefully soldered in place. Body is cracked below disc; holes and cracks in the disc itself; Herakles' knee flattened.
On the outside is an eight-petalled rosette surrounded by a band of alternating lotus and palmette. On the disc inside, in high relief, Herakles, seated on a rock covered by a lionskin with his quiver beside him, is approached by the priestess Auge. Incised with double lines in Greek characters above are the names *Auge* and *Delade*:

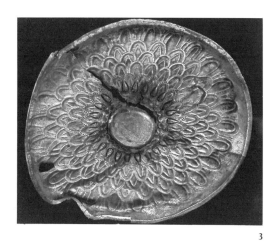

3

ΑΥΓΗ ΔΗΛΑΔΗ

On the rim, the Thracian personal name *Didykaimo*, also in Greek characters, is rendered in dots:

ΔΙΔΥΚΑΙΜΟ

4

5 Silver phiale
Diam. 8.1 cm; h. 6.5 cm
Inv. no. 22305
Body slightly misshapen, with tearing around the boss.
The body is of a slightly flattened globular shape, the neck conical and high. The rim is turned outwards and downwards. At the base of the neck is a raised band.

6 Silver-gilt phiale
Diam. 8.4 cm; h. 5.9 cm
Inv. no. 22306
Rim split; gilding partially missing.
The phiale has a globular body with low conical neck, the rim turned outwards and downwards. Around both the base of the neck and the boss are raised gilded bands.

7 Silver phiale
Diam. 9.4 cm; h. 6.1 cm
Inv. no. 22307
Well preserved.
The phiale has a flattened globular body and a short conical neck. The rim is drawn outwards and downwards. There is a decoration of three raised rings at the base of the neck.

8 Silver phiale
Diam. 9.0 cm; h. 6.3 cm
Inv. no. 22308
The body is of a flattened globular shape with a short conical neck.
The rim is drawn outwards. There is a raised ring at the base of the neck.

9 Silver phiale
Diam. 7.9 cm; h. 6.6 cm
Inv. no. 22309
The body is of a flattened globular shape with a high conical neck.
The rim is drawn strongly outwards and downwards. There is a raised ring at the base of the neck.

10 Silver phiale
Diam. 7.2 cm; h. 7.2 cm
Inv. no. 22310
The body is of a slightly flattened globular shape, the neck is conical and high. The rim is drawn outwards and downwards. There is a raised ring at the base of the neck.

11 Silver phiale
Diam. 7.7 cm; h. 6.8 cm
Inv. no. 22311
Preservation excellent.
The body is of a globular shape with a high conical neck. The rim is drawn outwards. There is a raised ring at the base of the neck.

12 Silver phiale
Diam. 9.2 cm; h. 6.3 cm
Inv. no. 22312
There is a break in the bottom.
The body is of a flattened globular shape with a low conical neck, the rim drawn slightly outwards. No decoration.

13 Silver phiale
Diam. 8.0 cm; h. 5.8 cm
Inv. no. 22313
The body is of a flattened globular shape with a low conical neck, the rim drawn outwards. No decoration.

9

14 Silver phiale
Diam. 8.8 cm; h. 6.1 cm
Inv. no. 22314
Well preserved.
The body is of a flattened globular shape with a low conical neck, the rim slightly drawn outwards. No decoration.

15 Silver phiale
Diam. 8.2 cm; h. 5.6 cm
Inv. no. 22315
Well preserved.
The body is of a semi-globular shape, the neck conical with the rim drawn outwards. No decoration.

16 Silver phiale
Diam. 9.6 cm; h. 7.3 cm
Inv. no. 22316
Excellently preserved.
The body resembles a flattened globe with a cylindrical neck. The rim is drawn outwards. No decoration.

17 Silver phiale
Diam. 7.9 cm; h. 6 cm
Inv. no. 22317
Body crushed before discovery.
The body is of a semi-globular shape with a high cylindrical neck. The rim is drawn slightly outwards. No decoration.

18 Silver phiale
Diam. 9.8 cm; h. 4.8 cm
Inv. no. 22318
Well preserved.
The body is of a very flattened globular shape, the neck conical with the rim slightly drawn outwards. No decoration. On the outside of the boss there is an incised sign resembling a double axe.

19 Silver phiale
Diam. 8.9 cm; h. 5.3 cm
Inv. no. 22319
Well preserved.
The body is of a flattened globular shape with a short conical neck, the rim drawn outwards. No decoration.

19

20 Silver phiale
Diam. 8.0 cm; h. 5.1 cm
Inv. no. 22320
Visible traces of hammering.
The body is of a flattened globular shape with a low conical neck, the rim drawn slightly outwards. No decoration.

21 Silver phiale
Diam. 9.1 cm; h. 5.1 cm
Inv. no. 22321
Well preserved.
The body is of a flattened globular shape with a low conical neck, the rim drawn slightly outwards. No decoration.

22 Silver phiale
Diam. 9.5 cm; h. 4.5 cm
Inv. no. 22322
Well preserved.
Shape as No. 21.

23 Silver phiale
Diam. 8.1 cm; h. 6.2 cm
Inv. no. 22323
Slightly crushed before discovery, with tearing and some holes in the body. Surface tarnished.
The body is of a globular shape with a short neck, the rim drawn outwards. No decoration.

24 Silver phiale
Diam. 8.7 cm; h. 6.3 cm
Inv. no. 22324
Crushed before discovery. Surface tarnished.
The body is of a globular shape with a high conical neck, the rim drawn strongly outwards. No decoration.

25 Silver phiale
Diam. 10.2 cm; h. 6.5 cm
Inv. no. 22325
Surface covered by incrustation and scratched before discovery.
The body is a semi-globular shape with a conical neck, the rim drawn outwards. No decoration.

26 Silver phiale
Diam. 12.3 cm; h. 3.2 cm
Inv. no. 22326
Well preserved.
The body is of a low and flattened globular shape with a cylindrical neck, the rim drawn strongly outwards. There is beading linked by tangents around the boss, which is surrounded by a multi-petalled rosette.

27 Silver phiale
Diam. 15.7 cm; h. 5.4 cm
Inv. no. 22327
Bottom cracked.
The base is of a flattened globular shape with a low conical neck. On top of the rim is a dotted inscription:

ΣΑΤΟΚ[Ω?]Ι

'(Property) of Satokos'

28 Silver phiale
Diam. 12.7 cm; h. 4.5 cm
Inv. no. 22328
Well preserved.
The body and neck are almost equal in height. On the outside under the rim is a dotted inscription:

ΚΟΤΥΟΣ ΕΞ ΒΕΟ

'(Property) of Kotys, from Beos'

29 Silver phiale
Diam. 20.0 cm; h. 5.5 cm
Inv. no. 22329
Crushed and cut before discovery.
On the outside under the rim is a dotted inscription:

ΚΟΤΥΟΣ ΕΓ ΒΕΟ ΔΙΣΛΟΙΑΣ ΕΠΟΙΗΣΕ

'(Property) of Kotys, from Beos, Disloias made (it)'

30 Silver phiale
Diam. 14.2 cm; h. 4.9 cm
Inv. no. 22330
On the outside on the short neck is a dotted inscription:

ΕΞ ΑΠΡΟ ΚΟΤΥΟΣ

'From Apros, (property) of Kotys'

31 Silver phiale
Diam. 13.5 cm; h. 4.2 cm
Inv. no. 22331
Well preserved.
On the outside, under the rim, is a dotted inscription:

ΚΟΤΥΟΣ ΕΞ ΑΠΡΟ

'(Property) of Kotys, from Apros'

32 Silver phiale
Diam. 14.7 cm; h. 3.6 cm
Inv. no. 22332
Two concentric bands are incised around the boss.

30

33 Silver phiale
Diam. 10.7 cm; h. 3.6 cm
Inv. no. 22333
Excellently preserved.
The body is unusually shallow and the rim is drawn strongly outwards. No decoration.

34 Silver phiale
Diam. 10.0 cm; h. 3.5 cm
Inv. no. 22334
Well preserved.
The body is shallower than the neck, which has the rim drawn strongly outwards. No decoration.

35 Silver phiale
Diam. 10.9 cm; h. 4.6 cm
Inv. no. 22335
Well preserved.
The body is almost identical in height to the neck. The rim is drawn outwards. No decoration.

36 Silver phiale
Diam. 10.5 cm; h. 3.9 cm
Inv. no. 22336
Holes and cracks in the body.
The base is unusually low and the neck relatively high. No decoration.

37 Silver phiale
Diam. 10.5 cm; h. 2.8 cm
Inv. no. 22337
Excellently preserved.
The neck is higher than the body. No decoration.

38 Silver phiale
Diam. 10.9 cm; h. 2.8 cm
Inv. no. 22338
Excellently preserved.
A ring of beading linked by tangents is raised around the boss. The body is decorated with broad radial fluting and elongated ovolo.

39 Silver phiale
Diam. 9.4 cm; h. 4.3 cm
Inv. no. 22339
Cracked around the boss.
Two ornamental bands are raised around the boss – an inner one of fluting and an outer one of elongated ovolo.

33

40 Silver phiale
Diam. 12.0 cm; h. 3.4 cm
Inv. no. 22340
Bottom of body split.
The body is fluted. On the outside under the rim is a dotted inscription:

ΚΟΤΥΟΣ ΕΞ ΒΕΟ

'(Property) of Kotys, from Beos'.
On the outside and around the boss is the graffito:

ΚΑΙΝΟ

41 Silver phiale
Diam. 14.2 cm; h. 4.6 cm
Inv. no. 22341
Well preserved.
Around the boss is a raised ring of tiny arcs encircled by a wide band of radial fluting. On the outside under the rim is a dotted inscription:

ΚΟΤΥΟΣ ΕΞ ΣΑΥΘΑΒΑΣ

'(Property) of Kotys, from Sauthaba'. On the boss are incised a pair of signs:

H H

42 Silver phiale
Diam. 14.8 cm; h. 4.6 cm
Inv. no. 22342
There is a hole in the bottom.
A human head in relief is soldered on the boss. Around it is a band of large leaves, arranged radially. On the outside on the neck is a dotted inscription:

ΚΟΤΥΟΣ ΕΞ ΑΡΓΙΣΚΗΣ

'(Property) of Kotys, from Ergiske'

43 Silver phiale
Diam. 13.2 cm; h. 5.2 cm
Inv. no. 22343
Well preserved.
Around the boss is a band of radial fluting; on the shoulder, a band of elongated ovolo. On the outside on the neck of a dotted inscription:

ΚΟΤΥΟΣ ΕΞ ΗΡΓΙΣΚΗΣ

'(Property) of Kotys, from Ergiske'

44 Silver phiale
Diam. 14.1 cm; h. 3.5 cm
Inv. no. 22344
Well preserved.
Alternating narrow and wide fluting are raised around the boss. On the outside, under the rim, is a dotted inscription:

ΚΕΡΣΕΒΛΕΠΤΟ ΕΞ ΕΡΓΙΣΚΗΣ

'(Property) of Kersebleptes, from Ergiske'

45 Silver phiale
Diam. 13.5 cm; h. 4.8 cm
Inv. no. 22345
Well preserved.
Radial fluting around the boss. On the outside, under the rim, are a scratched inscription (graffito):

ΚΟΤΥ

and a dotted inscription:

ΚΟΤΥΟΣ ΕΓ ΓΗΙΣΤΩΝ

'(Property) of Kotys, from Geistoi'

45

46

46 Silver phiale
Diam. 13.9 cm; h. 4.1 cm
Inv. no. 22346
Neck cracked.
Around the boss is a ring of circles linked by tangents; on the base, radial flutes. The shoulder is decorated with a band of elongated ovolo. On the outside, under the rim, is a dotted inscription:

ΚΟΤΥΟΣ ΕΞ ΑΡΓΙΣΚΗΣ
'(Property) of Kotys, from Ergiske'

47 Silver phiale
Diam. 11.5 cm; h. 4.9 cm
Inv. no. 22347
Well preserved.
There is graphite incrustation underneath the boss. A band of fluting alternating at the top with beading is raised around the boss. On the outside, under the rim, is a dotted inscription:

ΚΟΤΥΟΣ ΕΚ ΓΕΙΣΤΩΝ
'(Property) of Kotys, from Geistoi'

48 Silver phiale
Diam. 10.8 cm; h. 4.7 cm
Inv. no. 22348
Well preserved.
A ring of large beading is raised between two rings of incision around the boss.

49 Silver phiale
Diam. 12.4 cm; h. 4.6 cm
Inv. no. 22349
Well preserved.
Around the boss are two concentric rings of incision.

50 Silver phiale
Diam. 10.4 cm; h. 4.1 cm
Inv. no. 22350
Mouth cracked.
Around the boss is a ring of large raised beading, framed by bands of incision. On the base is a band of radial fluting. The shoulder is decorated with a band of elongated ovolo.

51 Silver phiale
Diam. 9.4 cm; h. 3.9 cm
Inv. no. 22351
Well preserved.
Around the boss is a band of radial fluting. The shoulder is decorated with a band of large enlongated ovolo.

52 Silver phiale
Diam. 8.7 cm; h. 4.0 cm
Inv. no. 22352
Body cracked with some holes.
The base is divided by incised rings into three ornamental bands of radial fluting.

48

53 Silver phiale
Diam. 10.6 cm; h. 3.8 cm
Inv. no. 22353
Well preserved.
A ring of circles with dotted centres and linked by tangents is raised around the boss. On the base is a band of radial fluting. A triangular sign is incised underneath the boss.

54 Silver phiale
Diam. 10.3 cm; h. 4.7 cm
Inv. no. 22354
Cracks in the body and around the boss.
The neck is taller than the body. Two rows of beading encircled by radial fluting are raised around the boss and there is a further band of fluting around the body.

55 Silver phiale
Diam. 9.4 cm; h. 2.8 cm
Inv. no. 22355
Excellently preserved.
The phiale is very shallow and the neck is equal in height to the body. Rings of pearls and incision, encircled by radial fluting, are raised around the boss. The shoulder is decorated with bands of elongated ovolo.

56 Silver phiale
Diam. 11.1 cm; h. 5.1 cm
Inv. no. 22356
Slightly cracked in six places.
Around the boss are two bands of incisions. The base is divided into two uneven bands of raised radial fluting. The shoulder is decorated with a band of elongated ovolo.

57 Silver phiale
Diam. 11.6 cm; h. 4.9 cm
Inv. no. 22357
Bottom cracked before discovery, with fragments missing; surface tarnished.
The body is almost conical in shape and is decorated with three bands of radial fluting.

58 Silver phiale
Diam. 10.5 cm; h. 4.8 cm
Inv. no. 22358
Split and cracked in two places.
A wide band of three rows of large beading is raised around the boss, followed by a band of radial fluting.

59 Silver-gilt phiale
Diam. 14.0 cm; h. 4.3 cm
Inv. no. 22359
Well preserved.
The boss, which is gilded, is framed by a ring of raised beading and the rest of the body is decorated with radial fluting with raised beads at the points of the flutes.

60 Silver phiale
Diam. 11.2 cm; h. 4.0 cm
Inv. no. 22360
Body cracked.
The phiale has a low neck, which has a ring of raised beading around the base. A ring of beading is also raised around the boss, surrounded by radial fluting.

61 Silver phiale
Diam. 10.0 cm; h. 3.8 cm
Inv. no. 22361
There is linear decoration around the boss and on the shoulder. The body is divided into two bands of raised radial fluting.

52

61

66 Silver phiale
Diam. 12.6 cm; h. 4.4 cm
Inv. no. 22366
Part of body missing.
The boss is framed by a ring of zig-zag lines and bands of radial fluting and elongated ovolo. On the outside, under the rim, are three dotted signs, two of them in the shape of a double-axe.

67 Silver phiale
Diam. 11.5 cm; h. 3.5 cm
Inv. no. 22367
Crushed and split before discovery, with a large part missing.
Around the boss is a wide band of radial fluting. The shoulder is decorated with elongated ovolo.

62 Silver phiale
Diam. 11.5 cm; h. 4.7 cm
Inv. no. 22362
Crushed and split before discovery.
Around the boss are bands of raised beading and radial fluting.

63 Silver phiale
Diam. 12.2 cm; h. 5.5 cm
Inv. no. 22363
Well preserved.
The boss is framed by two rows of incision and a band of radial fluting. The shoulder is decorated with a band of elongated ovolo.

64 Silver phiale
Diam. 15.6 cm; h. 5.2 cm
Inv. no. 22364
Well preserved, apart from a small hole in the body.
Around the boss is a band of raised radial fluting. The shoulder is decorated with a band of elongated ovolo.

65 Silver phiale
Diam. 11.5 cm; h. 4.8 cm
Inv. no. 22365
Well preserved.
Around the boss is a band of wide radial fluting. The shoulder is decorated with two concentric rings.

68 Silver phiale
Diam. 10.6 cm; h. 5.1 cm
Inv. no. 22368
Cracked around the boss and on the mouth.
Around the boss are two rings of raised beading and a band of transverse lines. The base is decorated with two bands of fluting and one of lines, the shoulder with a band of elongated ovolo.

70

69 Silver phiale
Diam. 12.3 cm; h. 3.9 cm
Inv. no. 22369
Well preserved.
Around the boss is a wide band of broad radial fluting.

70 Silver phiale
Diam. 9.9 cm; h. 2.8 cm
Inv. no. 22370
Well preserved.
Around the boss is a ring of large raised beading, encircled by a wide band of radial fluting framed by a ring of incision. The shoulder is decorated with a band of elongated ovolo.

71 Silver phiale
Diam. 13.9 cm; h. 4.4 cm
Inv. no. 22371
Well preserved.
The boss is encircled by a ring of incision and a wide band of raised radial fluting.

72 Silver phiale
Diam. 10.9 cm; h. 4.7 cm
Inv. no. 22372
Body cracked.
Around the boss are three bands of radial fluting of varying sizes.

73 Silver phiale
Diam. 10.8 cm; h. 4.1 cm
Inv. no. 22373
Slightly cracked.
On the body is a wide band of radial fluting framed by rings of incisions. On the shoulder there is a band of elongated ovolo.

74 Silver phiale
Diam. 11.2 cm; h. 4.3 cm
Inv. no. 22374
Well preserved.
Around the boss are three bands of elongated ovolo and transverse lines.

75 Silver phiale
Diam. 9.2 cm; h. 5.0 cm
Inv. no. 22375
Well preserved.
Around the boss are three bands of elongated ovolo.

76 Silver phiale
Diam. 9.8 cm; h. 5.5 cm
Inv. no. 22376
A large section of the bottom is missing.
Around the boss there is a wide band of radial fluting; on the shoulder, a band of elongated ovolo.

77 Silver phiale
Diam. 9.8 cm; h. 4.3 cm
Inv. no. 22377
Well preserved.
Around the boss are three bands of radial fluting.

78 Silver phiale
Diam. 8.8 cm; h. 4.0 cm
Inv. no. 22378
Cracked around the boss.
Around the boss are three bands of radial fluting.

79 Silver phiale
Diam. 13.9 cm; h. 3.9 cm
Inv. no. 22379
A section of the lip is missing.
Around the boss is a wide band of radial fluting. On the bottom there is a large cruciform sign.

80 Silver phiale
Diam. 11.1 cm; h. 4.5 cm
Inv. no. 22380
Body and lip cracked.
Around the boss are rings of ovolo and incisions surrounded by opposed bands, two of stylised palmettes.

81 Silver phiale
Diam. 17.0 cm; h. 3.3 cm
Inv. no. 22381
Well preserved; surface tarnished.
Around the boss are broad and narrow raised bands of alternating leaves and lotus buds.

81

80

82

82 Silver-gilt phiale
Diam. 17.9 cm; h. 3.6 cm
Inv. no. 22382
Body cracked and misshapen; rim jagged.
Around the boss are an inner gilded band of palmettes and an outer band of leaves and palmettes, which are alternatively gilded and plain.

83 Silver phiale
Diam. 14.8 cm; h. 4.1 cm
Inv. no. 22383
Well preserved.
Beneath the boss is a fifteen-petalled rosette, framed by a band of incisions; around it, two bands of palmettes alternating with almonds.

84 Silver phiale
Diam. 12.8 cm; h. 4.2 cm
Inv. no. 22384
Well preserved.
Around the boss is a band of scale-pattern resembling a fir-cone.

85 Silver phiale
Diam. 10.5 cm; h. 3.9 cm
Inv. no. 22385
Mouth cracked, with some holes.
Around the boss, a wide band of scale-pattern resembling a fir-cone between beading and ovolo.

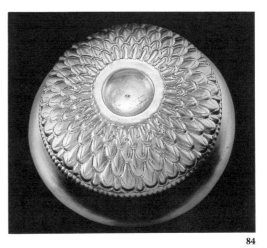

84

83

86 Silver phiale
Diam. 11.0 cm; h. 4.5 cm
Inv. no. 22386
Split before discovery. Mouth cracked and surface tarnished. Parts of the mouth and the bottom missing.
An eight-pointed star of narrow leaves radiates from the boss with a geometrical pattern of lozenges raised between.

87 Silver phiale
Diam. 11.8 cm; h. 4.9 cm
Inv. no. 22387
Crushed and split before discovery.
Around the boss is a scroll framing both small and large leaflike shapes. On the shoulder there is a band of stylised palmettes.

85

94

88 Silver phiale
Diam. 12.6 cm; h. 6.8 cm
Inv. no. 22388
A crack around the boss.
Around the boss is a scroll framing leaflike shapes.
On the shoulder there are two bands of ovolo.

89 Silver phiale
Diam. 12.1 cm; h. 5.8 cm
Inv. no. 22389
Well preserved.
Around the boss is a band of meanderform motif,
with two differing rings of ovolo on the shoulder.

90 Silver phiale
Diam. 12.1 cm; h. 6.7 cm
Inv. no. 22390
Split before discovery, with part missing.
Decoration as No. 89.

91 Silver phiale
Diam. 11.4 cm; h. 6.6 cm
Inv. no. 22391
Part of the body missing, surface tarnished.
Decoration as No. 89.

92 Silver phiale
Diam. 11.6 cm; h. 6.5 cm
Inv. no. 22392
Part of the base missing.
Decoration as No. 89.

93 Silver phiale
Diam. 11.6 cm; h. 4.5 cm
Inv. no. 22393
Split, with parts missing.
On the base is a continuous meanderform motif
with a band of ovolo on the shoulder.

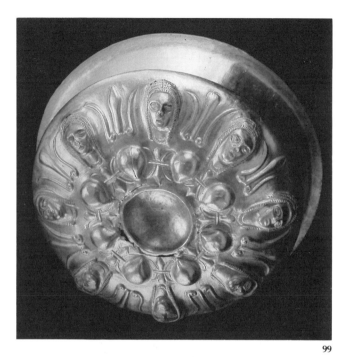

99

98

94 Silver phiale
Diam. 17.5 cm; h. 3.8 cm
Inv. no. 22394
Well preserved.
Around the boss is a band of six raised bovine heads alternating with acorns. Spirally curled tufts of hairs are chased on the foreheads.

95 Silver phiale
Diam. 17.6 cm; h. 3.8 cm
Inv. no. 22395
Cracked but otherwise well preserved.
Decoration as No. 94.

96 Silver phiale
Diam. 10.7 cm; h. 4.7 cm
Inv. no. 22396
Mouth and body cracked.
On the boss is a winged lion-griffin in relief. Around the boss is a band of palmettes alternating with stylised birds, their heads turned backwards.

97 Silver phiale   *See colour plates*
Diam. 18.8 cm; h. 4.0 cm
Inv. no. 22397
Body cracked; surface tarnished.
Amalgam-gilded; a rosette of fourteen units of leaf-and-dart, alternate leaves gilded, is framed by a ring of oblique incisions. The wide outer zone shows four pairs of confronted lion-griffins alternating with gilded palmettes. The lion-griffins are seated with their heads turned backwards. Each has one horn on its head and a triple wing on its shoulder.

98 Silver phiale
Diam. 10.5 cm; h. 4.1 cm
Inv. no. 22398
Mouth and body cracked.
Around the boss are eight rays with ends curling to the right. On the shoulder, elongated ovolo.

99 Silver phiale
Diam. 11.7 cm; h. 4.5 cm
Inv. no. 22399
Body and boss cracked.
Around the boss is a band of almonds and lotus buds in high relief. The outer zone shows eight female heads alternating with lotus buds. The hair of each head is in three braids falling beside the face.

100 Silver phiale
Diam. 10.8 cm; h. 4.4 cm
Inv. no. 22400
Well preserved.
Around the boss is a raised band of six stylised palmettes. The outer zone shows seven human heads, rendered in high relief. The locks of hair are curled at the ends. The eyebrows are thick, the eyes big.

101 Silver phiale
Diam. 12.4 cm; h. 3.9 cm
Inv. no. 22401
Central head cracked.
On the boss, in high relief, is a human head in full face, with short wavy hair. Around the boss there is radial fluting.

100

104

102 Silver phiale
Diam. 12.2 cm; h. 3.6 cm
Inv. no. 22402
Body cracked.
On the boss is a frontal human head in relief.
Around the boss there is radial fluting.

103 Silver phiale
Diam. 12.4 cm; h. 3.7 cm
Inv. no. 22403
Well preserved.
On the boss is a human head in high relief.
Around the boss there is radial fluting.

104 Silver phiale
Diam. 12.6 cm; h. 3.8 cm
Inv. no. 22404
Body cracked.
Around the boss there is a wreath of ivy,
surrounded by radial fluting.

105 Silver phiale
Diam. 15.7 cm; max. h. 4.8 cm
Inv. no. 22405
Mouth cracked; ancient rivetted repair.
Around the boss is a band of radial fluting.

106 Silver phiale
Diam. 14.2 cm; h. 7.0 cm
Inv. no. 22406
Crushed and ripped; surface tarnished.
Around the boss there is a wide raised band of four
large and very stylised palmettes. On the shoulder:
cross-hatching.

107 Silver phiale
Diam. 11.0 cm; h. 5.7 cm
Inv. no. 22407
Well preserved; no decoration.

108 Silver phiale
Diam. 10.5 cm; h. 4.5 cm
Inv. no. 22408
Small hole.
Around the boss are three bands of fluting.

109 Silver-gilt jug
H. 12.0 cm; diam. of mouth 5.6 cm, of body 7.0
cm, of foot 3.9 cm
Inv. no. 22409
Handle missing, but otherwise well preserved.
At the base of the neck is a raised ring of double
ovolo. The jug has a conical foot.

110 Silver jug
H. 15.9 cm; diam. of mouth 6.5 cm, of body 8.9
cm, of foot 4.4 cm
Inv. no. 22410
Handle damaged.
The handle is flat with a human head in relief on
the lower attachment. Two rows of ovolo are
raised around the shoulder and there is a ten-
petalled rosette underneath the foot.

111 Silver jug
H. 12.5 cm; diam. of mouth 7.1 cm, of body 8.0
cm, of foot 4.0 cm
Inv. no. 22411
Breaks in the lip.
There is a stylised palmette at the lower handle-
attachment. On the shoulder are a raised ring and
a band of ovolo.

112 Silver-gilt jug
H. 17.9 cm; diam. 12.6 cm
Inv. no. 22412
Crushed and damaged by the plough before
discovery. Handle and foot missing.
Ovolo in relief appear both at the base of the neck
and at the shoulder. On top of the mouth is a
dotted inscription:

ΚΟΤΥΣ ΑΠΟΛΛΩΝΟΣ ΠΑΙΣ
'Kotys son of Apollo'

113 Silver-gilt jug
H. 17.2 cm; diam. of mouth 7.0 cm, of body 9.5
cm, of foot 5.0 cm
Inv. no. 22413
Well preserved.
The jug handle is attached to the body by a silver
rivet. It rises high above the mouth and has a
palmette at the lower attachment. At mid-neck is
a raised band with incised decoration. There are
three bands of ovolo raised on the body and one
on the foot.

116 Silver jug
H. 10.4 cm; diam. of mouth 6.3 cm, of body 7.0 cm, of foot 4.4 cm
Inv. no. 22416
Mouth cracked.
The handle has two rows of ovolo and a palmette at the base. On the body are five similar bands of ovolo with dots at the tips.

117 Silver jug
H. 12.5 cm; diam. of mouth 6.0 cm, of body 7.4 cm, of foot 4.5 cm
Inv. no. 22417
Handle missing; surface tarnished; body repaired.
Four rings of ovolo as well as two bands of fluting are raised on the body.

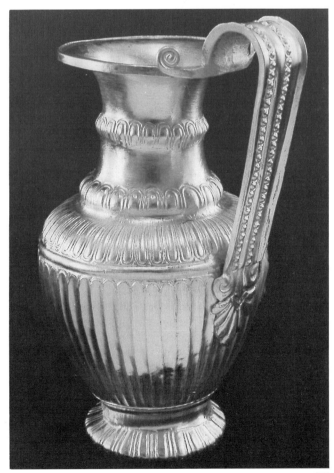

114

114 Silver jug
H. 13.5 cm; diam. of mouth 6.0 cm, of body 8.1 cm, of foot 6.8 cm
Inv. no. 22414
Part of the body split.
On the lower handle-attachment is a human head in high relief. At the base of the neck, there is a raised ring with oblique incisions; on the body, two bands of elongated ovolo.

115 Silver jug
H. 11.5 cm; diam. of mouth 5.3 cm, of body 6.6 cm, of foot 4.2 cm
Inv. no. 22415
Body cracked and partly missing.
The handle is decorated with two rows of raised beading and has a palmette at the base. There is a raised band of ovolo both in the middle and at the base of the neck, and also on the foot. A band of elongated ovolo is raised on the shoulder, and the body is fluted.

115

118 Silver jug

H. 12.7 cm; diam. of mouth 7.0 cm, of body 7.7 cm, of foot 5.2 cm

Inv. no. 22418

Neck slightly split.

On the shoulder are two wide bands of ovolo. The rest of the body is decorated by wide horizontal fluting. The handle is decorated with raised beading and bands of incisions. A twenty-six-petalled rosette is raised underneath the foot, with a graffito incised around it, including the word:

ΣΑΤΟΚΟ

'. . . (property) of Satokos . . .' (?)

119

118

119 Silver jug

H. 13.0 cm; diam. of mouth 7.1 cm, of body 7.8 cm, of foot 5.5 cm

Inv. no. 22419

Foot cracked; part of the applied decoration missing.

The handle terminates below in a palmette. The body is decorated by four bands of ovolo of varying width. A band of stylised palmettes and volutes was applied around the body.

127

120 Silver-gilt jug　　　*See colour plates*
H. 12.3 cm; diam. of mouth 7.0 cm, of body 8.2
cm, of foot 5.3 cm
Inv. no. 22420
Slightly cracked. Handle missing.
Gilding at base of neck. The decoration includes
bands of elongated ovolo, transverse lines and
upright fluting.

121 Silver jug
H. 11.2 cm; diam. of mouth 6.5 cm, of body 7.2
cm, of foot 4.5 cm
Inv. no. 22421
The foot is very badly split.
The handle ends below in a palmette. There is a
ring of ovolo at the base of the neck and on the
foot. The rest of the surface is decorated with a
wide band of upright fluting.

122 Silver jug
H. 10.9 cm; diam. of mouth 7.0 cm, of body 7.4
cm, of foot 5.2 cm
Inv. no. 22422
Bottom cracked.
There is a palmette at the base of the handle.
Rings of ovolo are raised at the base of the neck
and on the low foot. On the rest of the body there
are two bands of upright fluting.

123 Silver jug
H. 15.0 cm; diam. of mouth 8.0 cm, of body 8.5
cm, of foot 5.7 cm
Inv. no. 22423
Handle and parts of body and foot missing.
A ring of elongated ovolo is raised around the base
of the neck. On the body are bands of elongated
double ovolo of unequal height.

124 Silver-gilt jug
H. 11.5 cm; diam. of mouth 6.5 cm, of body 7.3
cm, of foot 4.8 cm
Inv. no. 22424
Part of foot missing.
There are three gilded bands of ovolo on the upper
body and two below. Around the middle of the
body is a band of leaf-like shapes, around which
winds a double line with incision.

125 Silver jug
H. 12.8 cm; diam. of mouth 6.0 cm, of body 7.4
cm, of foot 4.5 cm
Inv. no. 22425
Mouth and body cracked.
There is a palmette at the base of the handle. A
ring of double ovolo is raised around the base of
the neck. On the body is a broad band of leaves as
on No. 124.

126 Silver jug
H. 12.4 cm; diam. of mouth 6.3 cm, of body 7.4
cm, of foot 4.8 cm
Inv. no. 22426
Lower part of foot crushed.
The handle is decorated by bands of incisions and
there is a palmette at its base. A ring of ovolo is
raised around the base of the neck. On the body is
a broad band of leaves as on No. 125.

127 Silver jug
H. 10.0 cm; diam. of mouth 7.0 cm, of body 7.4
cm, of foot 4.7 cm
Inv. no. 22427
The jug stands on a low foot. There is a wide band
of elongated ovolo rendered on the shoulder with
two rings of incisions beneath. On the body is a
broad band of leaves as on No. 124.

128 Silver jug

H. 11.6 cm; diam. of mouth 7.5 cm, of body 8.3 cm, of foot 5.6 cm

Inv. no. 22428

Handle missing; mouth cracked; hole in foot.

It is similar in its decoration to No. 127. Only the two rings of incision are lacking.

129 Silver-gilt jug

H. 12.0 cm

Inv. no. 22429

Around the middle of the high neck there is a raised band with incision. A ring of cymation is raised both at the base of the neck and on the foot. On the body is a broad band of leaves as on No. 124.

130 Silver-gilt jug

H. 12.0 cm; diam. of mouth 5.5 cm, of body 6.6 cm, of foot 4.2 cm

Inv. no. 22430

Handle missing; some cracks.

The decoration is identical to No. 129.

131 Silver-gilt jug

H. 13.0 cm; diam. of mouth 5.7 cm, of body 7.1 cm, of foot 4.4 cm

Inv. no. 22431

Handle missing.

The decoration is identical to No.129

132 Silver-gilt jug

H. 12.0 cm; diam. of mouth 5.3 cm, of body 7.0 cm, of foot 4.1 cm

Inv. no. 22432

Body well preserved. Handle missing.

At the base of the neck is a raised ring of elongated ovolo above a ring of ovolo set horizotally; the latter is repeated at the base. Around the middle part of the body is a broad band, as on No. 124.

133 Silver jug

H. 12.7 cm; diam. of mouth 7.4 cm, of body 8.3 cm, of foot 5.3 cm

Inv. no. 22433

Well preserved.

Around the body there is a broad band as on No. 124. Three rings of ovolo are raised above it and two below.

130

134 Silver jug

H. 13.2 cm; diam. of mouth 6.0 cm, of body 7.4 cm, of foot 4.7 cm

Inv. no. 22434

Well preserved.

There is one ring of ovolo at the base of the neck and another on the foot. On the body there is a broad band as on No. 124. On the handle is a fourteen-petalled rosette.

135 Silver jug

H. 12.4 cm; diam. of mouth 5.9 cm, of body 7.0 cm, of foot 4.6 cm

Inv. no. 22435

Body crushed.

The decoration is identical to No. 134.

140

136 Silver-gilt jug *See colour plates*
H. 12.0 cm; diam. of mouth 5.9 cm, of body 7.3 cm, of foot 4.3 cm
Inv. no. 22436
Slightly crushed, with some gilding lost.
The decoration is similar to Nos. 134 and 135.

137 Silver jug
H. 12.7 cm; diam. of mouth 5.8 cm, of body 7.5 cm, of foot 4.5 cm
Inv. no. 22437
Well preserved.
At the base of the neck is a raised ring of ovolo. Around the body there is a wide band as on the preceding jugs, but framed above and below by rings of incisions.

138 Silver jug
H. 11.7 cm; diam. of mouth 5.1 cm, of body 6.2 cm, of foot 3.8 cm
Inv. no. 22438
Well preserved.
The decoration is identical to No. 137.

139 Silver jug
H. 13.3 cm; diam. of mouth 7.3 cm, of body 8.4 cm, of foot 5.2 cm
Inv. no. 22439
The round attachment at the lower end of the handle is decorated with a simple palmette. There are three rings of ovolo at the base of the neck and on the shoulder, and another on the foot. Around the body is a wide band as on the preceding jugs.

140 Silver-gilt jug
H. 11.5 cm; diam. of mouth 5.2 cm, of body 6.7 cm, of foot 4.0 cm
Inv. no. 22440
Handle palmette missing; surface tarnished.
At the base of the neck and on the shoulder are two rings of ovolo, arranged horizontally in the lower ring and framed by incisions. The body is decorated by a wide band as on the preceding jugs.

141 Silver-gilt jug
H. 11.3 cm; diam. of mouth 5.3 cm, of body 6.6 cm, of foot 4.0 cm
Inv. no. 22441
Well preserved.
The decoration is identical to No. 140.

142 Silver-gilt jug
H. 11.3 cm; diam. of mouth 5.1 cm, of body 5.9 cm, of foot 3.6 cm
Inv. no. 22442
Handle missing.
The decoration is similar to No. 141.

143 Silver jug
H. 14.0 cm; diam. of mouth 6.5 cm, of body 7.3 cm, of foot 4.4 cm
Inv. no. 22443
Foot crushed but otherwise well preserved.
At the base of the neck and on the foot there is a raised ring of cymation. The body is covered by leaves in relief alternating with raised triangles.

146

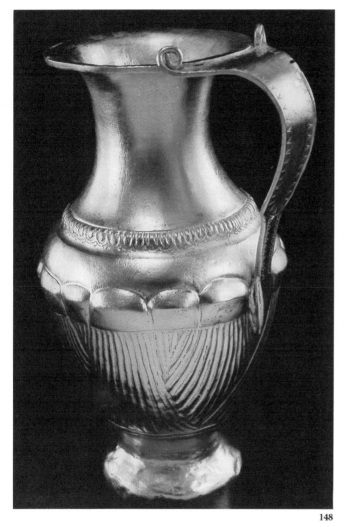

148

145 Silver jug   *See colour plates*
H. 13.0 cm; diam. of mouth 5.0 cm, of body 7.5 cm, of foot 4.7 cm
Inv. no. 22445
Body slightly crushed at the base. The jug was cast.
At the base of the neck is a raised ring of ovolo. Around the body, in high relief, there is a band of stylised leaves. At the base of the handle is a palmette.

146 Silver-gilt jug
H. 12.5 cm; diam. of mouth 5.2 cm, of body 7.1 cm, of foot 3.6 cm
Inv. no. 22446
Well preserved. The jug was cast.
The decoration is identical to No. 145, except that there is a stylised boar's head at the base of the handle. Its mane is rendered by incisions and both the snout and the eyes are in relief.

147 Silver-gilt jug
H. 11.6 cm; diam. of mouth 5.0 cm, of body 6.4 cm, of foot 4.2 cm
Inv. no. 22447
Well preserved.
The decoration is identical to No. 145.

148 Silver jug
H. 12.1 cm; diam. of mouth 5.7 cm, of body 7.0 cm, of foot 4.5 cm
Inv. no. 22448
Foot slightly crushed.
The decoration is similar to No. 145. Underneath the foot: a rosette.

149 Silver-gilt jug
H. 11.0 cm; diam. of mouth 5.5 cm, of body 7.0 cm, of foot 3.9 cm
Inv. no. 22449
Handle missing and part of neck broken away.
At the base of the neck, there is a raised band of ovolo.

150 Silver-gilt jug
H. 12.5 cm; diam. of mouth 6.0 cm, of body 7.4 cm, of foot 4.9 cm
Inv. no. 22450
Handle missing.
The decoration is identical to No. 148.

144 Silver jug
H. 12.7 cm; diam. of mouth 6.7 cm, of body 7.5 cm, of foot 4.7 cm
Inv. no. 22444
Bottom crushed and torn.
At the base of the neck is a raised ring of ovolo over a band of incisions, with another ring of elongated ovolo on the foot. The handle is decorated with two upright bands of ovolo with incisions between. There is a stylised palmette at the base of the handle. The body is decorated with a band of leaves, turning at the top into stylised capitals.

151 Silver jug
H. 11.6 cm; diam. of mouth 6.6 cm, of body 7.4
cm, of foot 4.9 cm
Inv. no. 22451
Mouth split and foot deformed.
Around the base of the neck is a raised ring of
ovolo. On the body, a band of highly stylised
leaves with longitudinal fluting. The handle is
decorated with two upright bands of ovolo and
terminates at the base in a palmette.

152 Silver jug
H. 13.1 cm; diam. of mouth 7.2 cm, of body 7.8
cm, of foot 4.5 cm
Inv. no. 22452
Mouth and body torn.
The decoration is identical to No. 151.

153 Silver jug
H. 11.0 cm; diam. of mouth 6.7 cm, of body 7.3
cm, of foot 4.2 cm
Inv. no. 22453
Handle missing; body split in the middle and neck
detached. The decoration is identical to No. 152.

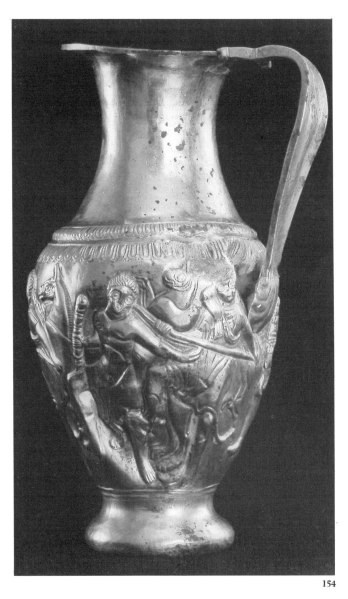

154

154a

58

155

154 Silver jug

H. 14.3 cm; diam. of mouth 6.0 cm, of body 7.5 cm, of foot 4.4 cm

Inv. no. 22454

Cracks and holes in the body and mouth. Body misshapen and handle reattached. Surface tarnished.

At the base of the neck are two raised rings of ovolo. The handle ends in a stylised palmette. Underneath the foot is a sixteen-petalled rosette. Around the body is a wide frieze showing a scene from the struggle between Herakles and the Amazons. The hero is shown young and naked, holding a club in his right hand, while with the left he is defending himself from an attacking Amazon. Behind the hero is the forepart of a lion-griffin. The Amazon, wearing a knee-length tunic, moves vigorously to the left with a spear in her hand. The forepart of a horse is shown behind her. The identical scene is repeated three times.

155 Silver-gilt jug   *See colour plates*

H. 13.5 cm; diam. of mouth 7.8 cm, of body 8.5 cm, of foot 5.1 cm

Inv. no. 22455

Well preserved, surface tarnished.

At the base of the neck, and on the foot, is a raised ring of ovolo. The handle is decorated with incisions between two upright bands of ovolo, and ends below in a human head in relief. On the body the Great Goddess is shown, armed with bow and arrow and seated sideways on a lioness. The group is repeated (facing in the opposite direction) on the other side of the jug. A lion attacking a stag is seen between the two representations of the Goddess.

156 Silver-gilt jug

H. 13.0 cm; diam. of mouth 5.5 cm, of body 7.4 cm, of foot 4.0 cm

Inv. no. 22456

Handle loose at the top. Body slightly misshapen.

At the base of the neck is a raised ring of ovolo. The handle is decorated with fluting and ends with a palmette. On each side of the body there is an identical representation of a lion, which has sprung up on the back of a hind and has bitten its prey in the neck.

156

157 Silver jug

H. 12.0 cm; diam. of mouth 8.5 cm, of body 8.3 cm, of foot 5.1 cm

Inv. no. 22457

Well preserved.

Rings of ovolo and beading appear at the base of the neck and on the foot. The handle ends in a palmette. On the body, in unusually high relief, are two four-wheeled chariots each drawn by four winged horses. Each chariot has a female charioteer and a passenger. One of the passengers is the Great Goddess, holding a branch and a *phiale*. The other has a bow and arrow, and may represent the Great Goddess again or her consort.

158 Silver jug

See colour plates

H. 11.5 cm; diam. of mouth 7.3 cm, of body 8.0 cm, of foot 4.5 cm

Inv. no. 22458

Mouth split; handle repaired; body cracked; surface tarnished.

At the base of the neck is a ring of ovolo over a ring of incisions. The handle terminates below in a palmette. The body is divided by rings of incisions into two zones, the upper one wider. In the centre of the upper frieze, a standing winged goddess, seen in frontal view, holds a dog by its paws in each hand. The dogs' heads are turned backwards. From each side two winged monsters resembling centaurs approach the goddess. On the lower frieze a bull on its knees is attacked from each side by a pair of dogs.

157

158

159

159 Silver-gilt jug
H. 12.5 cm; diam. of mouth 5.9 cm, of body 7.7
cm, of foot 4.6 cm
Inv. no. 22459
Neck twisted.
The mouth is pulled outwards and turned downwards to form a rim in which is a raised ring of
ovolo. There are four more similar rings below,
two on the neck and two on the foot. The handle
is decorated with engraved bands of incisions and
has a female head with braids in relief at its base.
A similar head is added below the base of the
handle. On each side of the jug is a horseman with
a spear in high relief. Between the hunters is a
boar wounded in the neck with a spear.
Underneath the foot is a ten-petalled rosette.

160 Silver jug
H. 11.0 cm; diam. of mouth 5.9 cm, of body 6.3 cm
Inv. no. 22460
Well preserved.
At the base of the neck, and on the foot, is a raised
ring of ovolo. A band of ivy leaves, framed by rings
of incisions, is chased on the shoulder. On the
body there is a wide band showing two stylised
palmettes with volutes resembling horned animal-
heads. On each side of the volute stands a stylised
scaly animal with a curly tail. The handle
terminates below in palmette.

159a

161 Silver-gilt jug

See colour plates

H. 12.7 cm; diam. of mouth 6.5 cm, of body 7.6 cm

Inv. no. 22461

Crushed and split in several places.

The ornaments and the images are similar to those on No. 160, except that the band of ivy leaves is lacking and the ornaments are gilded.

162 Silver jug

H. 13.5 cm; diam. of mouth 6.7 cm, of body 8.5 cm, of foot 4.5 cm

Inv. no. 22462

Handle missing. One side of the jug is split with a piece missing.

At the base of the neck, and on the foot, is a raised ring of ovolo. Underneath the foot, a thirty-petalled rosette. On the shoulder, in high relief, is a row of thirteen rams' heads shown frontally. On the body, there appears to be a representation of the struggle between Bellerophon and the Chimaera (both figures damaged). Between them appears an eagle-griffin with wings and a tail ending in a snake's head. There are two stags below, a lioness behind, and in front a bird holding a snake in its beak.

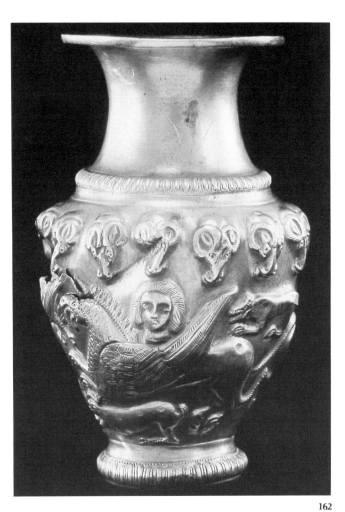

162

162a

163 Silver-gilt kotyle   *See colour plates*

H. 9.4 cm; diam. of mouth 8.5 cm, of body 6.3 cm, of foot 2.9 cm

Inv. no. 22463

Both handles missing.

The cup was raised. The body is conical with the rim drawn outwards. It was originally provided with a pair of upright handles soldered to the upper part of the body. A wreath of four interlinked ivy sprigs is engraved under the rim. The ornament is gilded.

164 Silver-gilt skyphos   *See colour plates*

H. 7.1 cm; diam. of mouth 7.4 cm, of foot 4.0 cm

Inv. no. 22464

One of the handles is missing. The bottom is broken.

The cup was cast and is in the shape of a classical *skyphos* with two round handles set horizontally. Beneath the foot is a twenty-petalled rosette. Beneath the rim, which is turned outwards, and on the foot, is an incised ring of ovolo. On the body, there is a wide frieze with six stylised palmettes, each placed upon a pair of S-shaped scrolls. Beneath the ornament are three rings of ovolo and incision. The decoration is gilded.

165 Silver-gilt beaker   *See colour plates*

H. 20 cm; diam. of foot 11.7 cm; max. diam. of mouth 13 cm

Inv. no. 22465

The cup was badly crushed and torn by the plough before discovery, and pieces of the rim are missing.

The beaker was originally biconical in shape, tapering towards the waist (*cf. Fig. 4*). On the base is a wide band of inverted scale-pattern over rows of ovolo, chevrons and palmettes. Beneath the rim, there is a continuous motif resembling antlers terminating in birds' heads. Around the body is a frieze of animals, all seen in profile, facing right: a bird of prey with a long horn or crest holds a fish in its beak and a hare in its talons; in front are a goat and then a stag with long antlers, its head missing. Finally, a composite creature with a stag's antlers, a goat's beard and eight legs with uncloven hooves. The head and antlers are missing, but similar monsters appear on biconical beakers of the same kind found in Romania.

Suggestions for further reading

Dimitrov, D. P., and Čičikova, M., *The Thracian City of Seuthopolis* (BAR, supplementary series, 38, 1978)

Fol, A., and Marazov, I., *Thrace and the Thracians* (1977)

Hoddinott, R. F., *Bulgaria in Antiquity* (1975)

Hoddinott, R. F., *The Thracians* (1981)

Venedikov, I., *Thracian Treasures from Bulgaria* (British Museum Exhibition Catalogue, 1976)

Venedikov, I., and Gerassimov, T., *Thracian Art Treasures* (1975)